If It Weren't For People

MANAGEMENT
Would Be A Science

Marshall Mc Murran

ENGINEERING & MANAGEMENT PRESS
a division of the Institute of Industrial Engineers
Norcross, Georgia

ENGINEERING & MANAGEMENT PRESS
© 1998 Institute of Industrial Engineers

Cataloging-In-Publication Data

Mc Murran, Marshall
    If it weren't for people, management would be a science/by Marshall Mc Murran.
        p.   cm.
    ISBN 0-89806-210-1
    1. Management--Anecdotes. 2. Organizational behavior--Anecdotes. 3. Executive ability--anecdotes. I. Title.
    HD31.M3859   1998
    658--dc21   98-38649
                                                           CIP

Printed in the United States of America

02   01   00   99   98   1   2   3   4   5

Cover Design: Craig Hall

ISBN 0-89806-210-1

Quantity discounts available

For additional copies, contact:
ENGINEERING & MANAGEMENT PRESS
IIE Member & Customer Service
25 Technology Park, Norcross, GA 30092
770-449-0460 phone
770-263-8532 fax

www.iienet.org

Contents

To Lisa

To Max & Mary –
Thank you for helping
me get a good start
Mac

Preface

THE MANY IDIOSYNCRASIES OF PEOPLE make being a manager both fascinating and difficult. Good managers should be continually creating order from chaos; yet, even great managers often find themselves generating little eddies of chaos without meaning to. This book is directed toward identifying and suggesting corrections for some of these management mistakes. If you, the reader, find the tenets offered here valuable, I hope that you vigorously pursue the preferred forms of the suggested changes despite the inevitable pressures to desist and retreat to the old ways. With perseverance, you should find improving conditions in the shop, laboratory, and office, coupled with improving financial returns.

I have been fortunate enough to have been associated with a number of outstanding executives and managers. They directed successful endeavors that were completed as they had been planned, came in near or under budgeted costs, and were finished on time. These successes were often achieved despite roadblocks placed along the way by a number of chaos creators, some of them other senior managers. My thirty-five years of experience has served to adjust, but not substantially change, my early views of the causes of some of the more telling management shortcomings. As I learned, developed, modified, and applied the guides and principles discussed here, I recognized a marked improvement in my ability and that of my reporting managers to deal effectively with people and problems. Upon examination of today's management practices, I find that the application of several of the management principles I learned and honed over the years is not yet widespread. I hope that will change.

The discussions of situations used here are taken from real experiences, some slightly modified to avoid embarrassing members of the cast. These stories are intended to dramatize, entertain, and emphasize important points. Each chapter deals with a separate issue. The suggestions offered can, for the most part, be put into practice piecemeal. However, you will have better results by adopting all those you think to be applicable to your business. Most of the important ideas are in bold print throughout the book.

Let's now discuss some of the common mistakes that many managers have made, that more managers will likely make, and that some managers are surely making now.

– Mac Mc Murran

Acknowledgments

I would like to thank the following folks for their invaluable help with the writing and editing of the manuscript. Jeff Schmidt, Vice President, Engineering, Rockwell International, now retired, who critiqued portions of the manuscript and supplied information about the goings-on at North American Aviation shortly after World War II. Thanks are also due to members of the Mc Murran family for their encouragement and support: to Professor Bret Mc Murran who reviewed the manuscript; to Professor Shawnee Mc Murran for her support; to Teresa Quinn, Assistant Department Head, Scientific Computing and Communication, Lawrence Livermore Laboratories, who critiqued Chapter 9 and supplied source information concerning the ASCI program; to Greg Mc Murran, Chief Investment Officer, Analytic-TSA for his critiques and comments; and to Grant Mc Murran for his help identifying source information at the Drucker Library. Finally, I would like to thank Ms. Delia Wilson of Winnipeg, Canada for her detailed review of the second draft, and Mr. R. M. du Plessis presently of Tustin, California for his biting critique of portions of the third draft.

I also wish to thank Scott Adams for allowing the use of some of his Dilbert cartoons.

Any errors of commission or omission are mine.

CHAPTER 1

A Bit of History

"May you live in interesting times."
– Old Scots curse

BEFORE WE TAKE THE PLUNGE into the body of this work, it may be worthwhile to consider a brief and selected history of management thought, together with some observations of recent influences on management style. Before the Industrial Revolution, management as we think of it today was almost an unknown art. (The art of organization has been with us since the dawn of time. We have good evidence of the ancients' effective organizational abilities in the existence of the Pyramids, the Great Wall of China, and other massive construction projects that survive today.) It is unlikely though that the kings, generals, pharos, and khans gave much thought to the motivation and welfare of the masses of laborers and artisans who built their projects. It wasn't until the eighteenth century that anyone besides executives in the churches, governments, and military thought much about managing people in groups. Few of the organizations existing up to that time were particularly efficient, except in the sense that the Roman legions were efficient.

Britain changed from an agrarian economy to the world's first industrial nation when the early mechanized looms went to work in the 1760s. Once started, the Industrial Revolution burgeoned, fueled by invention. Gas lighting, stationary steam engines, Bessemer steel processes, and locomotives are but a few examples of the useful tools employed during this technology explosion. In the beginning, the revolution brought local prosperity to some of the larger cities, but these mechanical innovations and their derivatives also displaced workers, producing centers of unemployment. The resulting human unrest and associated social ills were often dealt with severely by the authorities. The British government and the rising industrialists tended to work hand in glove, with the objective of keeping the working classes in what was supposed to be their "place." Although not officially sanctioned, their place was expected to be mostly poor, often hungry, and always dependent on the industrial barons for their livelihood. Owners and overseers of the period would have dismissed out of hand any of today's notions about worker welfare or motivation as the product of dangerously warped and jellied minds.

Modern management thought pretty much began after the Industrial Revolution was underway. There were few important works prior to that time. Nicoli Machiavelli and his incisive, short management work, *The Prince*, was certainly one. While intended as princely advice and not as a management guide, it should be on the must-read list of all managers. Even so, most writings before the 1880s dealing with management-like subjects are useful to us principally as historical documents. The works of people like Erich Roll (1775-1805) discussed some relatively modern management techniques, but such writings were rather few and far between. Charles Babbage (1792-1871), of calculating engine fame, had a number of things to say about management around 1832, but his works are of limited use today. Babbage must have been an irascible soul, and therefore well-suited to write about management of the time. A contemporary of his wrote, "He spoke as if he hated mankind in general, Englishmen, in particular, and the English government and organ grinders most of all."

During the mid 1800s, management works were often unintentionally supplemented by social writings by the likes of Charles Dickens, who alone, doubtless had a larger readership and greater influence on the public conscience than all of the management-related works put together.

Works of folks like Max Weber (1864-1920), of the Protestant work ethic, give us a sense of the thought of the time. An American, Fredrick Taylor (1856-1915) is generally given credit for being one of the first proponents of so-called "scientific," or as he preferred, "task" management. Taylor dealt in some measure with the underlying psychology of behavior, but he appears from his writings to have espoused industrial engineering somewhat more than business management. Chester Barnard (1886-1961), who was an orthodox thinker; Henry Gantt, who was a somewhat unorthodox thinker, known for the Gantt chart; and Frank Gilbreth are generally given credit for nurturing industrial engineering in America. All influenced management thought of the early 1900s in mostly positive ways by stimulating readers to think about improved work methods, worker environment, and to a degree, worker motivation.

For 150 years or so after the start of the Industrial Revolution, short-term economics ruled. Factory owners spent as little as possible on worker comfort and safety. Working conditions ranged from cold and dangerous to hot and dangerous. Most industrial workers had only a rudimentary education. While this limited knowledge tended to be common for the time, it suited the plant owners to a tee. "Skilled" workers typically had learned only a narrow single skill during their apprenticeship. Most workers had only shank's mare for transportation. Moving to a new job, if the opportunity ever presented itself, meant leaving friends and relatives for a new home, an unpleasant prospect. Factory owners quickly caught on to the idea that they had essentially a captive work force and treated the workers accordingly, increasing hours and ratcheting down pay whenever opportunity arose.

When a competing plant was built near to an established factory, it was generally done to use available energy sources and take advantage of the labor pool. Often the owners would agree on a wage and hour pattern for the area over a tankard of ale, stifling competition for the available labor force. Even so, the owners were continually looking to implement techniques designed to reduce incipient work force mobility. It was during this time that the notion of the company town was born, ostensibly to provide better living conditions for the employees. More often than not, it was used to indenture families to the plant owners, sometimes for generations. Most management philosophies continued to be based on the premise that the employees were simple, and that sometimes surly folk wanted firm guidance from their betters. Forelock tugging was expected.

Some of the following pithy quotes from intellectuals and industrialists of the day serve to give a flavor of the views managers and economists held of the worker.

Adam Smith: "The man whose whole life is spent in performing a few simple operations...naturally loses, therefore, the habit of (mental) exertion, and generally becomes as stupid and ignorant as it is possible for a human creature to become..." (In Smith's defense, he was almost certainly talking about the downside of labor specialization. Nevertheless, it is a sad commentary on his view of the human condition. Particularly, when he has the deserved reputation of being the principal liberal economist of his time.)

Anon: "It is a fact, well known...that scarcity...promotes industry. A reduction of wages in the woolen manufacture would be a national blessing and advantage, and no real injury to the poor. By this means, we might keep our trade, uphold our rents, and reform the people in the bargain."

Pollard, on the Quaker Lead Company's war against employee moral depravity: "The drive to raise the level of respectability and morality among the working classes was not undertaken for their own sake, but primarily...as an aspect of building up a new factory discipline."

Mantoux, on early industrial entrepreneurs: "...hard, sometimes cruel, their passions and greeds were those of upstarts. They had the reputation of being heavy drinkers, and of having little regard for the honour of their female employees. They were proud of their newly acquired wealth and lived in great style with footmen, carriages, and gorgeous town and country houses."

It was only after skilled labor was found to be in occasional short supply that anything like modern management thought evolved. Wages for some of the more skilled trades became competitive. Working hours, while not always shorter, at least became more predictable, and the relationship of managers and plant employees became an issue. Workers' guilds, associations, and unions became forces for management to reckon with.

These labor organizations persisted despite the efforts of management and governments to rein them in before they became strong enough to do harm to the bottom line. At first, these groups had limited objectives, principally those of forcing the redressing of local grievances by the strength of numbers. Many folks today like to think that ours is an enlightened era, and the need for organized labor is becoming a thing of the past. But anyone who doubts the need for the odd labor union to keep the worst of management in check should spend a little time in an operating coal mine. Safety costs money. Because there was no unified pressure on management, the inherent dangers of mining killed many early minors. Unfortunately, bargaining groups have their own penchants for occasionally doing bad things to their members. It is an imperfect world.

The poor social and economic conditions of most workers during the Industrial Revolution spawned groups whose objective was the sharing of this new wealth among everyone. These were the "new" Socialists. The Marxists came shortly after the Socialists. Often they were the same people.

As the nineteenth century drew to a close, European socialist organizations were growing rapidly. They were soon electing their candidates to national legislatures. Socialism and Marxism sent chills through Europe's governments and business leaders, so much so that well before the

Russian revolution, the various establishments were taking repressive measures against both the Socialists and Marxists. Meanwhile, Marxism was becoming the dominant ideology of European socialism, and worse, had taken on an international view (Workers of the World, Unite!). In 1914, the advent of World War I provided a setback to the international communist movement, proving beyond much doubt that nationalism was still alive and well, despite Marxist doctrine.

The War to End All Wars

One of the least publicized facts of World War I was the miserable performance turned in by American industrial contractors in support of that war effort. At the beginning of the United States' entry in this "war to end all wars," America's industrial barons promised to produce whatever the U.S. military might need. An early promise to provide more than 20,000 aircraft "to darken the skies of Europe" never came to pass. Not one airplane of American design fought in the war. Of some 2,200 artillery pieces used by the American Expeditionary Force, only about 100 were produced in America. Tank production by the vaunted American auto factories was even more dismal. Twenty-three thousand tanks were ordered. Only twenty or so had been accepted by war's end. American-built weapons and ammunition were always in short supply and badly flawed.

American industrialists arranged to build the British de Haviland DH-4 under license. This was a proven aircraft design that did not push the state of any art and should have been a snap to build. Unfortunately, virtually every American-built DH-4 aircraft upon arrival in Europe was found to require rework and repair. When the rework was complete, they were still dangerous to fly. They had fuel tank problems. The DH-4s burned a lot. They were called "flaming coffins" by those unlucky enough to fly them.

Many promises were made by American industry. Few were met. War profiteering seemed the rule of the day. The military officers on the receiving end of this shoddy treatment took note.

During ten or so years following the World War I armistice, most sectors of the U.S. economy were booming. The introduction of new fabrication and assembly techniques brought lower production costs of automobiles and other hard goods. The assembly line was one of the more important and innovative developments. The line put specialized workers directly into the creation of pieces of products in real time. The man who had earlier introduced the assembly line was Ransom E. Olds, for whom the REO and Oldsmobile cars were named (not Henry Ford, as many believe). In 1901, Olds was able to manage a sixfold increase in production using his repetitive assembly line techniques. This dramatic productivity improvement wasn't lost on Henry Ford, who was a quick study. By adding a conveyor belt system, Ford was able to reduce the time needed to build a Model-T Ford from about one and one-half days to something like ninety minutes.

Driven by the demand for worker efficiency (read "speed"), Frank and Lillian Gilbreth began about 1910 to study the effect the degree of human movement had on productivity. They codified human actions, assigning a numerical value to each one studied. The goal of assembly-line management was efficiency and efficiency was generally had, but at the peril of dehumanizing workers. Charlie Chaplin's silent film, *Modern Times*, graphically parodies working conditions of that era. Management would try to increase production by keeping workers at their stations, and on occasion, surreptitiously speed up the lines. While the production line's advantages over craft construction and fabrication are well known, these advantages aren't free. The line has several shortcomings. Probably the worst of these faults is that the failure of any single station can shut down the entire line. This undesirable feature focused strict managerial insistence on timeliness and attendance of factory workers. Management has since provided for relief operators, robots, and parallel assembly lines to mitigate this problem, but it hasn't gone away. Other problems with production lines that continuously need fixing are worker boredom, the spreading of responsibility for quality among several people, the endless need to balance the input to work in progess, and the rather large start-up and shut-down costs.

During his administration, President Calvin Coolidge proclaimed that "the business of America is business." Even so, precious little was spent by anyone on any kind of product research. The U.S. technology engine was sputtering. Jobs were becoming progressively harder to get, although the stock markets kept reaching new highs. Communism became an unwanted force in the workplace. Management generally took a hard line with the workers, holding to the notion that "if some of them quit, there are plenty more in the hiring halls."

With the arrival of the near worldwide depression of the 1930s, misery came to workers and managers alike. By 1933, 25 percent of the U.S. labor force was without work. Stocks had lost 80 percent of their peak value. The union organizers were busy. Helped by the National Labor Relations Act of 1935, ranks of union workers grew from three million to ten million (virtually all were men). Management and union leaders became adversaries. **Not unlike today, neither side seemed to understand that the ultimate goals for both sides were identical.**

Meanwhile, back with the U.S. military, there was little available money to spend on weapons development, let alone anything as ethereal as research. The few military goods ordered barely sustained the small standing force. The little ongoing national research was mostly accomplished by bright, often strange young men in their garages and by academics. One or two forward-looking large companies funded research laboratories. Bell Laboratories is perhaps the prime example. Begun in 1925 as a combination of a pair of smaller laboratories, Bell Labs was made autonomous at the outset of its existence, allowing the engineers and scientists to focus on research, instead of being dragged into day-to-day production problems.

When new war clouds loomed over Europe in the mid 1930s, it was clear to high-ranking military officers that all U.S. military services would soon be placing orders with U.S. suppliers. The services would need new and prototype weaponry as well as large quantities of munitions and armaments for existing designs. The junior officers of World War I were now colonels, generals, and admirals. They had remembered well the treatment of the U.S. military at the hands of American industry during that war. It was no wonder these officers now felt that they had to assume stringent control over their contractors, using military models of management, exercising this control quickly and decisively before things got out of hand again.

I submit for your consideration a postulate that gives governments in general, and the U.S. military/government establishment in particular, a great deal of credit (or blame) for many of the management practices that today permeate the business entities of the world. I believe there is much more blame than credit to be assigned to this military influence on nonmilitary organizations.

The Influence of WW II

Soon after Pearl Harbor, federal laws were rapidly put into place to influence the behavior of the U.S. civilian population. Rationing and price controls were introduced. U.S. commercial activity was placed under various degrees of government control. Companies that refused to cooperate, or were slow to do so, were seized "for the duration." A graphic study in *Life* magazine of a scowling Sewell Avery being carried from his executive office at Montgomery Ward, by a pair of helmeted soldiers, reflected the mood of the time. The United States was engaged in a merciless struggle with particularly heinous enemies. Patriotic fervor was at a high pitch. For most people, the government could do no wrong. The military way was not only the right way, it was often the only way.

From 1942 to the end of the war in 1945, the U.S. military and its bureaucratic civilian cousins influenced everything imaginable. To save cloth (or possibly to improve military morale) skirt hems were ordained higher, and cuffs disappeared from trousers. Hairnets called "snoods," made of yarn were introduced in the factories to keep the longer hair of the women workers out of the machines. These snoods immediately found their way into general fashion. For the first time in the United States, large numbers of women went to work alongside men in production areas.

A major migration of workers from Middle America to the coastal defense plants caused permanent population shifts to these areas. During this entire period, workers and managers alike were strongly influenced by the military view of how things should be run. It all worked in that production rapidly increased until the United States truly earned the oft-used title, "The Arsenal of Democracy." No one said things had to be efficient. Problems were solved by throwing people and money at them. Strikes were outlawed. Anyone who bucked the trend or complained about bad management was reminded that "there is a war on."

People were grouped and supervised according to their separate skills. These functional groupings have always appeared to be easier to manage than multi-skilled organizations, but they tended to lack a cohesive purpose. Functional managers' priorities were directed to the accomplishment of assigned short-term goals. These managers were not usually motivated to sift through the available project information to make informed decisions concerning project priority and quality issues. Focus was brought to major weapons programs by breaking the large functional crowds into smaller pieces. Each of these groups was assigned to a different program managed by a single, usually senior, executive. Smaller or less important activities were left in a sort of organizational limbo. During this period, good managers were hard to come by. A lot of them were fighting overseas. The country wasn't yet ready to accept women managing men. Anything that permitted lower skilled management to be thrown into the breach was considered a positive good.

At the end of World War II, many of the ex-officers and noncommissioned officers became supervisors and managers in rapidly expanding companies producing civilian goods to meet worldwide demand. They brought with them the ideas of management learned while in the service of their country. As these companies further expanded, these people rose in the companies' hierarchies. Meanwhile, ongoing congressional reviews of military procurement practices during "The War" revealed some glaring problems. Pricing practices, particularly for spares and support equipment, were held highly suspect. Contracts too often seemed written to favor the contractor. The military's answer was now that the war was over and the pressure was off, both it and the civilian contractor management could become more "businesslike." Along the way, a few leftover wrongdoers were punished.

For a few years after World War II, and before we found ourselves facing tough global competition from two of our old enemies and the odd friend, we enjoyed a near-monopoly in production of hard goods. This situation was particularly prevalent in the so-called "high tech" industries (transport aircraft, autos, data processing, instrumentation, weaponry, and the like). It was seen to a lesser degree in pharmaceuticals, chemicals, medical hardware, and metal fabrication. After World War II, the American factories that had produced the surfeit of war materiel were unscathed, while many of the factories of our prewar competition lay in ruins. With global competition weak, U.S. factories rapidly shifted from the production of war materiel to the supply of consumer goods to recovering world markets. This supply became a flood, substantially aided by Uncle Sam's largesse in providing recovery money to the stricken people of Europe and Asia. With much of this money flowing back into the U.S. to purchase U.S.-made goods, manufacturers in the United States could sell about anything they could produce somewhere in the world. Efficiency and productivity were given a few passing thoughts, but by and large, there was no motivation to change anything as long as products could be made available and the sellers' market stayed intact.

At the same time, the United States military was trying to recast itself into a new and leaner organization. The top brass were trying to convince themselves and Congress that they had gotten religion, had rejected the extravagances of war, were adopting "sound modern management practices," and seeing to it that their contractors did the same. During the immediate postwar period, officers' training routinely included courses on principles of management drawn up by civilian consultants. These teachings were often treated as gospel, but they varied widely in their value, ranging from the naive and inapplicable to the useful. The result was a new generation of procurement officers who believed that they were competent to control and manage commercial organizations. These people would direct the procurement of military-funded research and the resulting complex weapons systems during the massive cold war arms build-up to come.

It should be emphasized here that the rules for military management are simply not applicable to competitive businesses. Given its mission, the military has no choice but to be an essentially wasteful entity. This statement is not intended as a castigation of military management practices. Rather it recognizes preparation for war and the execution of the military mission for what it is. Supplies, equipment, and munitions are obtained in the hope that they will never be used in anger. When new materiel and weapons are found to support the military mission of the time, they are procured in quantities dictated by the perceived threat. The older stuff is sold to the highest bidder or thrown away. If war breaks out, little thought is given to the general conservation of available resources, only to success in battle. As all successful commanders point out, "You've got to expect losses."

Military management philosophy is based on the premise that command and control must be authoritarian. "Do exactly as I say and do it now" is the only form of direction that is likely to work well in combat. Dissension, even intelligent dissension, is definitely not rewarded. "Better" ways of doing things are evaluated in the light of the effect on combat readiness, with peacetime cost savings well down the list in importance. The military should never try to emulate industry, or vice versa. However, military influence on industrial organization and management practices came in earnest during World War II, continued into the Korean and cold wars, and reached a local peak during the Vietnam period. Even so, neither the peacetime nor the wartime mode of military operation represents a model than can be successfully applied by industry.

American forces were still on their way home from World War II when the specter of a communist-dominated Europe arose once again, with our recent Soviet ally the principal culprit. While we were trying to figure what to do about all that, Asia began to rumble. In 1949, China became a communist power almost overnight. For a brief time we were able to hide behind our perceived atomic shield, but in June of 1950, the communist North Korea invaded the South. We took our ships out of mothball cocoons, dusted off our World War II equipment, called up the reservists, and went back to war.

During the Korean police action, management of arms production was initially handled in what the military considered the new businesslike fashion, but frayed edges began to show that hadn't been evident during World War II. There were fewer controls in place over civilian behavior. Rationing was over. Local shortages appeared. Profitable civilian production of hard goods was booming. The Korean police action wasn't nearly as popular a conflict as World War II. As the North Koreans marched down the Korean peninsula in spite of everything we were able to do, the military was accused by the media and by the public of the sin of unpreparedness. The pre-Korean military policy to become more frugal and businesslike was shelved. As a result, rigid controls were imposed on military suppliers, setting the stage for times to come.

Armies went up and down the Korean peninsula like yo-yos, finally reaching a stalemate of sorts near the 38th parallel where the whole thing began. It all ended in an orgy of military activity that the Air Force called Operation Rat Killer, which immediately preceded the Armistice of July 1953. With the Korean conflict out of the way, the United States Congress turned its full attention to rooting out the dreaded communist in our midst. Military procurement contracts by the thousands were canceled. Factories returned to the production of consumer goods. The U.S. population bought and furnished tract houses and had babies.

The weapons' procurement front was fairly quiet until Sputnik beeped overhead in 1956. Then we panicked. At the behest of Congress, the United States military began pouring money into the procurement of gadgets of all sorts to close the technology gap. The Soviets were using huge liquid-fueled rockets to throw big things into orbit around Earth. We had nothing of the kind, so we poured money into rocket engine development programs to provide us with the capability of throwing things at the next continent. To be useful, these powerful rockets had to be augmented with computers, guidance and control systems, and tons of support equipment.

The lack of effective global competition, coupled with unprecedented demand in the immediate postwar world had already made production quality and efficiency secondary to meeting demand in most U.S. industries. Now, the new military requirements further stressed the production capacity of U.S. industry. As a result, sales flourished but these burgeoning sales still had little to do with operating efficiencies. In spite of this, **the business successes during the 1950s and 60s were taken as proof that all was being managed correctly. Accepted structures and management systems of the time were thought to be "validated." These models are still being used in today's businesses and are classic examples of nonsequiturs.**

There was a temporary decline in military influence over industry in the late 1960s caused by the vocal unpopularity of the Vietnam war. "Down with the military-industrial complex!" echoed from ivy-covered walls throughout the country. Even MIT students rioted. Among other acts of vandalism, these future engineers made a concerted attempt to close Draper Laboratories (the Draper people were developing inertial sensors destined for ballistic missiles).

Well before the student riots, though, the military had been working diligently to tighten its hold on major technology segments of American industry by continually adding to the management controls already in place. New contracts were written with very specific clauses. In order to control suppliers, management systems and organizations within contractor companies were directed to parallel those of the military. The infamous "C Spec," which required the reporting of costs and progress in excruciating detail, embodied a number of these invasive practices. The military encountered little resistance. Most suppliers saw no great benefit in suggesting that many of the required practices were expensive and generally yielded poor results. After all, this would only lead to friction. Besides, military customers were quite willing to pay for the adoption of their preferred control procedures whether they worked or not.

At that time, more than a few of the larger government contractors already had organizations and practices in place that had evolved through their long-time military contacts. These contractor organizations were roughly parallel to those of the military and required only modest continuous change to keep them in line with the latest military directives.

One of the poorer innovations put in practice in the 1960s was the program management hierarchy as an overlay to the usual functional organization. This so-called matrix management required functional managers of engineering, marketing, and quality assurance groups to attempt to satisfy two bosses. They had to satisfy their own supervisors who signed their salary reviews and the program/project manager who didn't, but who had the ear of upper management and was responsible to the military customer for contract performance.

The very idea of reporting to more than one boss goes against basic biblical training. According to **St Matthew 7:24, "No man can serve two masters: for either he will hate the one and love the other; or else he will hold to the one, and despise the other...).**" This quixotic matrix scheme almost certainly stems from a rational observation that programs and projects need people managing them who feel responsible for the success or failure of these important entities.

Just as the functional managers of the World War II factories had limited oversight, so do the functional managers of today have little real sense of the relative importance of the programs, projects, and products they are supporting. Yet, these are the people assigning operating priorities, generally without much guidance. Assumed functional priorities may or may not be in the best interests of the company. Program-oriented people are much better positioned to decide where assets are to be best applied to their programs. Unfortunately, the genius that came up with the matrix idea forgot about equating responsibility and authority.

The structures, accounting systems, and personnel practices of giant companies that may have only one or two of their many divisions devoted to military sales (e.g., General Motors, General Electric, Ford, etc.) have been influenced by the military. Even though most of the output of these large companies is directed to nonmilitary ends, these organizations have generally adopted military-approved accounting systems. The accounting system in one large company (almost certainly in others as well) was designed around the requirement to collect sufficient cost data at the end of each work week to justify the instant billing of the U.S. government for progress payments. This almost real-time accounting created a myriad of problems in collecting accurate audited costs for commercial products, but the system persists to this day.

It's interesting, but distressing, to observe that we lost our competitive edge in shipbuilding, photographic equipment, and ferrous metal refining soon after the Korean War. Major losses soon followed in auto manufacturing, light aircraft manufacturing (lost principally through our insistence that the aircraft manufacturers assume near-unlimited liability for the product), and electronic equipment production/assembly. This is all rather surprising when one considers that the engineering and production skills required in these industries are the very same as in those where we are still preeminent. The rationalizations for all of this presented from time to time include "ridiculously high American wages," "an excessively strong dollar," "excesses of labor union demands," "the presumed (for a while) superiority of the Japanese worker," and "adverse effects of all the nasty safety and environmental protection laws on product costs." While some of these conditions added to the cost of American products, industry did little to put its own house in order. **Management is better advised to spend time identifying and correcting problems within their purview rather than fussing about things they can't control.**

A spate of employee unease coming from rather diverse quarters has arisen recently. Much of this bother seems to be related to our practice of American-style management. Management hasn't done particularly well in articulating and quantifying the causes of these problems (let alone finding solutions), seeing only the symptoms that range from strikes to sickouts to employee lawsuits. Unless one searches diligently, root causes tend to be obscured by complexity and sometimes by wishful thinking.

Rather than addressing some of the more dimly lit causes, many companies go for the advertised easy and quick solution. Management is bombarded by suggestions of how best to improve relations with employees, and how to increase efficiency, sales, profit, and anything else that seems amenable to improvement. Copious seminars, books, audiotapes, and now CDs are available to advise the concerned manager. Much of this material treats symptoms, not causes. Discussions with operating managers indicate that precious little of the advice given in seminars and the like ever finds its way into practice. Even good advice often goes by the board. For example, John Young's excellent recommendations while chairing President Reagan's Commission on Industrial Competitiveness were generally ignored by Mr. Reagan and friends. Mr. Young, the CEO of Hewlett-Packard at the time, took a leave of absence from his job in order to create and oversee a project that he strongly believed to be worthy of executive consideration. He was understandably disappointed to see nothing of substance done with the suggestions of his committee.

It is hard to understand why so many people continue to commission studies, papers, and seminars promising to create paths leading to better

things, and then opt for changing nothing or make a faltering attempt to change, fail, and then repeat the process.

It seems likely that some of these continuing failures are due to the emperor's new clothes syndrome. **Once the teachings of a consultant or group have gained respectability, it becomes heresy to observe that this wisdom may not apply or might be wrong. The common belief is that failure to reap the promised benefits must be the fault of the people trying to make it all work. The contents of these teachings should be critically examined before casting blame on the students.**

Only a few years ago, when the Japanese were eating our collective lunch in the automotive and electronics industries, a substantial number of books and training courses touted the benefits of emulating Japanese management styles. Most of the suggested innovations were variations on the theme of cementing group loyalties. Attempts to make over the way American employees behaved generally came a cropper, with the possible exception of the introduction of quality circles. (Even these circles can be dangerous if they aren't tightly managed to prevent them being used as forum to pick at local supervision.) Since all this yielded little or no benefit, most of the champions have, by now, quietly slunk away. Most American managers no longer feel a burning desire to copy the Japanese ways, and for good reason—the American and Japanese cultures are quite different. The Japanese culture gives top marks to group loyalty and frowns on individualists, particularly those people who are low in the pecking order. We Americans usually adopt a more individual and free-wheeling style, although we also tend to dismiss good ideas coming from those lower in our pecking order.

This cultural difference has probably been a major contributor in the inability of the Japanese to create cutting edge computer programs and to design (as opposed to produce) innovative computing equipment, even though Japanese engineers are arguably among the best in the world.

Some time ago, I was in Japan to assess the value of a redesigned micro-processor that was being offered for sale or trade by Mitsubishi Industries. The microprocessor was a modified 6502, based on the device that was the heart and soul of the pre-Macintosh Apple computers. This new version was touted by Mitsubishi as a dramatic improvement over the old part. The new design offered many more active operation codes than were to be found in the original 6502. On closer examination, though, it turned out that all but two of the many new codes were redundant. It was hard to understand why anyone would change a design to provide several different ways to control the same addition operation.

When I questioned the Mitsubishi engineers about this odd design change, I found that the programmers had little say in the functional design of the devices. They were considered a cut or two beneath the electrical engineers in the hierarchy at Mitsubishi. The electrical engineers had the design authority. The senior electrical engineer, who was a very mature individual with no apparent software background, had directed that all available code spaces be used up in the easiest way possible. What, if anything, the new operation codes accomplished was apparently of little importance to him, as long as there were a lot more of them. When the programmers reviewed the design, they had politely suggested that these heretofore unused codes be used to control new functions that would be truly useful in programming the new processor. They were politely rebuffed. The programmers politely accepted the decision although it was patently the wrong thing to do. It isn't likely that a team of American programmers worth their salt would have given up so easily or given up at all. (Since there are very few, if any, absolutes in this world, it is worth noting that not all Japanese programmers follow in the footsteps of those in the story. Turn Iwatani, a programmer, invented the PAC MAN game while working for Namco Ltd. of Japan. Recent computer graphics developed and refined by Japanese programmers and engineers at Japanese companies are outstanding.)

Meanwhile, back in the United States in the late 1990s, driven by the emergence of stiff global competition, the often soul-searching evaluation of American business practices goes on apace despite a self-serving tendency to validate a lot of old bad habits. Unfortunately, management techniques that did not work well in the 1950s through the 1980s are still being recommended and applied near the turn of the new century, with about the same degree of success enjoyed earlier. In the recent past, we have seen long periods of seemingly daily downsizing of loyal staffs in the name of competitiveness, not to mention the layoffs resulting from an urge to merge. While the recent economic strength has slowed layoffs and spurred a dramatic addition to the nation's work force, insecurity and dissatisfaction among workers are still indicated in the results of recent polls. There is a resurgence in the militancy of bargaining organizations. I fear that management is still failing to garner the trust of the people they manage.

There are many ways to organize. None of them should be vague and confusing. Why rely on procedures and policies in such volume and detail instead of face-to-face management? Why plan in so much detail for such long periods, and then neither believe nor follow the completed plans?

The influence of government goes far beyond the effects of regulation and taxation policies, although these are influential enough. Government/military entities are large and free-spending customers. As such, they should be well-treated by their suppliers, but this treatment should not extend to allowing the government customer to reform company structure or to peruse the deeper secrets of the company at will. **No customer should be allowed to dictate the manner in which a supplier company conducts its lawful business.**

Despite all the over-detailed, long-range planning done by almost every large company in America, management tends to avoid long-term solutions, opting instead for a perceived short-term good.

There are a lot of organizational models extant, but to my knowledge, there are no complete models of truly product-structured organizations available today for inspection by the inquiring manager. New, small companies come into being because someone thinks he or she has found a product or service that is superior to those available.

Virtually all these new entities are structured to focus on the one thing that is important—the company's product or service. **Start-ups today tend to be more effectively managed than older, larger firms but as the successful start-ups grow, they often migrate to the functional structures of the older and larger businesses.** These less-than-effective migrations occur because there is an available existing model describing a known quantity. "If it's good for AT&T, it must be good for small businesses as they grow." Is it really good for AT&T, or is AT&T the way it is because top management is reluctant to initiate meaningful changes as long as the stockholders are reasonably well-behaved and the modest profits continue? Mature companies are often run by people who have a personal stake in the lack of change. Many of these executives feel, probably correctly, that significant change will adversely affect their pay.

With our vaunted technological base, we have been unable to plan and manage any new and cost-effective public transportation system in the last half of this century. Public surface travel both locally and nationally is poorly used, and with the minor exception of long-distance bus lines, requires continuous government subsidies to keep operating at all. I suggest that **many of the problems plaguing our government, our public transportation system, and our research laboratories are the same resource management problems confronting industry.**

We have not learned enough from our mistakes. Congress and the U.S. military have not yet perceived that the armed services and quasi-military organizations such as the CIA, NSA, and the FBI are not well-served by continual attempts to emulate the bureaucratic perception of industry, just as industry is poorly served by adopting things uniquely military. Even so, U.S. industry is presently favored with a reputation of having the most productive work force in the world. Unfortunately, in the process, we have chosen to abdicate several of our earlier preeminent positions. **Think what we could do if we chose to do more things right.**

CHAPTER 2

No Man Can Serve Two Masters

"Confusion now hath made his masterpiece!"

Macduff — from *Macbeth*

Matrix Management Doesn't Work Well

FUNNY-STRANGE ORGANIZATIONS POP UP continually, often resulting from nothing more than fuzzy thinking while emulating other existing structures. Sometimes these new troublesome organizations are created to satisfy an odd management impulse to adjust the nest. **At the first sign of trouble, some managers move organizations about with little thought of probable consequences, transmogrifying reporting structures willy-nilly in the somewhat forlorn hope that the new sum of the shuffled parts will turn out to be greater than the prior whole.**

DILBERT reprinted by permission of United Features Syndicate, Inc.

Many of these officially recognized organizations get in the way of good management, particularly when reporting relationships are muddied through the reluctance of the organizing manager to make difficult decisions. When this occurs, established structures tend to be ignored by the better managers. A series of useful informal relationships spring up, based on friendship and mutual respect, having little to do with the organizational charts. The savvy managers know whose word can be trusted and whose organization can accomplish promised objectives despite the way things are organized. The occurrence of this sort of organizational anarchy, even though it may work for a time, should be sufficient evidence to the responsible executive that things need putting right.

The Watchdog of Stony Mount

It was early spring in Southern California. Major changes in the organization and management of the Stony Mount Aerospace Company were about to bloom along with the California poppies. Unfortunately, these impending changes were prompted by customer dissatisfaction. The military overseers of the largest program at Stony Mount—the Watchdog Ballistic Missile—were fed up with the apparent lack of response of the company to Air Force direction. For this reason, a small army of Stony Mount managers was about to partake of one of the ever-popular tools of modern management science, an "off-site meeting."

Stony Mount had been a very successful airplane builder during World War II. At war's end, Stony Mount management had decided, correctly as it turned out, that the company's future lay in establishing new engineering expertise in modern weapons technologies, while maintaining the company's position as a prime aircraft contractor. This meant adding several new technical disciplines to the company's repertoire including rocketry, digital computing, and missile guidance.

Stony Mount management knew how to organize and control the design and building of airplanes. Each aircraft project was assigned to a separate and devoted entity created for that purpose. The principal aeronautic design team reported to the airplane project manager. There were central functions that were not part of the team (some drafting, some housekeeping, and the like), but seldom were there any serious conflicts among design teams for these shared resources. The Navy and the Army Air Corps (later the Air Force) could get satisfaction from a project/program manager who was clearly in charge. There were only a few active aircraft projects at any time and the management was relatively simple.

Guided and ballistic missile design was different. Design and development of these complex systems were performed by several large and specialized engineering groups often located at a distance from each other, both physically and intellectually. Each separately managed group worked on a principal subsystem; computer, inertial measurement unit, flight controls, engine, airframe, or support equipment. Design of these subsystems was an involved task, mostly lacking the body of prior knowledge that was available to the designers of a new, but evolutionary, airplane.

Missile research and development organizations were typically structured by function (engineering, manufacturing, quality, and so on). These functional organizations could be easily thousands strong. The successful aircraft design teams had now been replaced by several diverse, technologically rich organizations attacking the frontiers of knowledge, but lacking focus. Because of the diversity of assignments within a functional organization, the military procurement people often had trouble finding anyone in charge to complain to. When the military representatives ran across someone with authority that would listen, they generally got a polite rebuff. The functional managers all had pieces of several programs to worry about. They were not about to promise satisfaction to a single procurement officer at the expense of all others.

Competing missile programs, each with essentially the same design goals, were often funded for two or more contractors. The higher levels of the military establishment based redundant contracting on the somewhat fuzzy idea that if one design house couldn't find successful solutions, another one might. Somehow out of all this would come the weapons to preserve the peace. It worked, but not well, and at an unnecessarily high cost.

Compounding the organizational difficulties were military rules for safeguarding sensitive (classified) information. Where the government classification and protection rules didn't get in the way, various company policies with similar aims did, which created redundant research and design efforts and inflated the need for engineers. The upshot was that from the mid-1950s through the 1960s, anyone who could justify the title of engineer was a sought-after commodity. Many of these people were unknown quantities to their immediate supervisors. Some were just unknown. Engineering supervisors were overworked, often to the point of accepting any warm body with the hope that the new employee might accomplish something useful and help take off the pressure. Hiring goals were established, and those were generally number goals, not quality goals.

I was fortunate in that era to have had a boss who insisted on a measure of quality in our new hires. **As one of our basic selection criteria, we used good undergraduate grade point averages (3.5 out of 4.0, or better, when there was a surfeit of applicants).**

As missile programs evolved, systems became ever more complex. Not surprisingly, a number of design flaws and launch failures surfaced. As a consequence, the military took action. With the duel objectives of reducing the design burden on a single contractor and making the job of military contract management easier, the military intentionally limited contractor responsibilities. Operating policies evolved that discouraged a single company from bidding on the design, development, and management of an entire complex weapon system. This practice quickly led to an unforeseen sticky problem. There was now no lead or prime contractor for major weapons systems, including Watchdog. On aircraft programs the airframe contractor had always been the prime or general contractor. One of the more important jobs of the prime contractor was to manage other contractors and suppliers working on the project. In the case of Watchdog and similar programs, the missile airframe contractor was in no position to manage the engine, computer, or guidance people. The engine people were not right to oversee the computer designers or the aerodynamicists. There was really no contractor to act as prime, so the military came up with an odd solution. They awarded contracts to a number of associate primes. With several companies participating as equals on the Watchdog program, the military contracts and procurement people were the only ones having the authority to manage and coordinate the work among these diverse organizations. This was a job the military folks were not capable of handling. So, after a false start or two, the military hired another contractor as a systems manager, who had no direct authority over the other contractors, but was supposed to manage them.

This all worked about as well as anyone would expect. The military, though, had begun to rely on the technical expertise of these systems people, so they couldn't just disappear. Instead, the role of the systems manager was altered to that of military advisor. Funding was essentially unlimited. Large engineering staffs and think tanks emerged. Once these systems houses got their respective noses into the weapons systems tents, many of them used their beefed-up staffs to act as *ex officio* systems managers with the tacit approval of the military. Some used the information they gained in their advisory capacities to compete with the existing hardware contractors. This fuzzied things up even more.

The stage was now set for serious schedule problems at Stony Mount. All three military services were under tremendous pressure to field nuclear delivery platforms at the earliest possible moment. Funding was not a limiting factor. There was a surfeit of business. Stony Mount pre-prototype and prototype computers were designed into Watchdog, as well as several other systems destined for the armed services. Contracts had been awarded to the Stony Mount inertial guidance division for several different configurations of guidance systems scheduled for use in diverse applications. Similar situations existed at the flight control and engine divisions.

The specific purpose of the off-site meeting was to spring a predetermined program/project management concept on the Stony Mount managers while maintaining all of the usual functional organizations. Once heard, it took some doing to convince any of the attendees that the Stony Mount top brass was serious. Unfortunately, they were. They had already agreed with the Air Force to add the overlay that was soon to be dubbed "matrix management." The Stony Mount president opened the session with a brief pronouncement saying, "What you are about to hear is the price of staying on the Watchdog program. It has my full support." The management consultants hired to explain it all failed dismally. Although, to give them their due, only those who were experts in defending indefensible points could have succeeded.

The argument used by the consultant to justify the coming changes went something like this: "Because Stony Mount has no central manager save the President with sufficient authority to direct the Watchdog program, the Air Force contracts people feel they aren't getting the proper attention from the Stony Mount functional management. The Air Force wants a focal point at Stony Mount wholly devoted to the Watchdog program who is able to control all of the people working on Watchdog."

The Air Force liked the way airplane designs were managed at Stony Mount, but it wanted an airplane program organization. The Air Force worried that forcing Stony Mount to completely reorganize would cause upheaval at a critical time and that any problems would ultimately find their way back to the Air Force doorstep. However, if Stony Mount took on the program organization voluntarily, the Air Force would not be culpable.

The choices were clear. The only other possible alternative to the proposed matrix was to reorganize Stony Mount and put everyone working on Watchdog into a large Watchdog organization. This change could be accomplished with some pain and would have to be carefully time-phased. The overworked line engineers composing the bulk of the functional work force were already timeshared among several important military programs. If most of them were instantly merged into Watchdog, admirals and generals responsible for other weapons programs would threaten Stony Mount with contract cancellations.

The consultant droned on concluding with this: "Stony Mount must have both a strong central Watchdog management team reporting to the highest levels of Stony Mount management and a strong functional management team. The Watchdog program manager's office will have the authority to direct the functional people working on Watchdog. The strong functional management team will have complete control of their people and will make all of this work smoothly." Say what?!

The formal meeting ground to an end. The participants adjourned to the host bar to lick their wounds and discuss what they thought they heard. Amid predictions of doom and threats of quitting, the organizational problem was addressed. The basic problem was the authority dichotomy. **A secondary concern was that details of ongoing research and devel-**

opment could now be dictated by the Air Force procurement staff by way of the program managers following a "do it our way but meet the specification" philosophy.

Various organizational alternatives were suggested, outlined, and discarded. One well-supported position recommended that Stony Mount walk away from the Watchdog program. There was more than enough work for everyone without it. This alternative, of course, did not appeal to the Stony Mount president.

There were a few other suggestions. The functional organizations could be recast as resource pools, assigning people to the various programs and projects as needed. But how would the few people remaining in the pools be funded as the workload varied? All auditors, military or otherwise, take a dim view of supporting people who aren't working gainfully now but might be needed sometime later. It was argued that perhaps Stony Mount could retain all projects except Watchdog on the functional side. After all, Watchdog was the biggest single contract at Stony Mount, but there were still the timesharing problems that wouldn't go away.

To confuse things still further, project managers already existed in the Stony Mount engineering department. They were called project engineers when they weren't called something else. They acted for the Chief Engineer's office, focusing engineering effort on specific projects. This was an earlier admission by engineering management that functional organizations had their shortcomings. It was an attempt on a small scale to do what the Air Force was about to force all of Stony Mount to do on a grand scale, and for about the same reasons. So the engineering department had already had a sip of matrix management. Most functional people looked on the project engineering organizations as intrusive and superfluous, but these project engineers did some real good. This hybrid engineering organization worked better than a purely functional one, but relied on brotherhood to operate. At least someone was watching the programs, and there was never any real question that functional management was responsible for the designs and people.

The project engineers present at the off-site meeting were naturally concerned about what was planned for them once the program management matrix was put in place. When the large Watchdog program office was formed, what would happen to the project engineers? As it turned out, nothing. There would be yet one more management crowd that would have to figure how best to deal with all the others.

A contract administration organization unique to Watchdog had been previously formed at Stony Mount. It had been growing steadily and inexorably from inception. It would soon be the nucleus of the Stony Mount Watchdog program management office. The Watchdog administrators had already assembled a good-sized work force. By meeting time, there were perhaps 400 people working on central kinds of things that had been duplicated or transferred from the line organizations. However, the bulk of the Watchdog work would always be done, sometimes redundantly, by the thousands more working in the various functional divisions, although the program management organization grew to more than 1,500 people at the height of the Watchdog activity.

Reluctantly those who had attended the meeting accepted that they had no choice but to give matrix management a try. To put the best face on it, they observed that they were after all part of American industry, and they could do anything if they put their minds to it. Not really, but at the time no one knew better.

Stony Mount had plenty of company. Other military contractors working on a myriad of programs soon suffered the same fate. As things evolved, all large military design and development programs would be directed to do something similar for similar reasons.

Matrix management came down with a vengeance. Over the next few years, Stony Mount muddled through with varying degrees of difficulty. Program managers tried everything. They sunk to cajolery. They used the top management club freely. They bypassed the functional managers and harassed the staffs. A few program managers believed they were selected by a divine power and could do no wrong. Others developed King Kong personalities.

An adversarial relationship rapidly formed between the functional and program people. The program managers quickly became uniformly disrespected throughout the functional ranks even though many were sound people. Since they were charged with representing the interests of Watchdog, these program managers were very unsympathetic with anything that appeared to them to be less than complete cooperation for whatever reason. They were particularly upset where their problems were caused by the functional managers trying to meet commitments on other projects or programs. The functional managers soon learned to give lip service with honest, wide-open eyes and straight faces. They lied, stole, and yielded to pressure by finding shortcuts that may have seemed satisfactory at the time, but often just pushed the problems downstream.

The program managers had their operating difficulties as well. They were generally not expert in the technology they were managing, so the engineers pulled the wool over their eyes. The poor program managers had to stand up and be slapped about for technical, schedule, and cost overrun problems by both the Air Force and by Stony Mount top management. Program management routinely repeated as truth information received from the functional staff without being able to judge the quality. The program managers were overloaded with responsibility and underwhelmed with authority. Careers zoomed or were smashed on a whim, floorshow, or chance.

The whole thing cost a pretty penny. The salaries of the new army of program managers were significant, but the organizational inefficiencies resulting from multiple and overlapping management were more costly. Unfortunately, these massive and superfluous costs are now hidden for all time. The perception from the top down was that things were made somewhat more orderly. Response to Air Force direction appeared to be improved. Air Force management had someone to talk to who listened. Parochialism seemed to be blunted. The Air Force customer felt that things were better, so the change stuck to the bitter end. The added costs be damned!

Other programs at Stony Mount adopted matrix management either for self-preservation or from the unfounded belief that it really made things better. To this day, matrix management is found in organizations throughout the country. **Matrix management may offer what appears to be an easy and effective compromise solution to problems similar to the** ones described above. Rest assured that it does not! There is always a better way. The better way may well offer some short-term heartburn along with the solution, but it also offers an opportunity to create a better and more effective lasting organization.

Focus vs. Function

Today we find matrix structures taking many forms. We find them used to combat unclear relationships between the engineering and marketing groups, between the engineering and manufacturing groups, between the marketing and manufacturing groups, and between the marketing and sales groups, to name a few. Government is rampant with complex matrices. Multiple government entities routinely try to assume authority over each other. Often these intentionally contentious relationships are used to justify odd accommodations involving some form of matrix management, while each side tries to gain control.

Both government and industry are composed of far too many organizational entities, with their overlapping spheres of authority and responsibility. Rather than go through the effort to fix the basic problems, management continually resorts to brotherhood, band-aids, and matrices. Research laboratories typically have management difficulties in spades. Highly competent technical people can be prima donnas. Rather than step on these powerful egos, management often elects to allow the researchers to do as they choose—for a time. Once things get out of hand, a matrix organization is formed to restore order without doing anything too definite that could trigger violent disapproval from some of the more volatile researchers.

A bad management idea has recently emerged in yet another attempt to fix the matrix problems. This latest foray involves the use of project/program teams that have been temporarily split from the basic functional organization. These teams are expected to be the entities that do and focus the work, working around and through the remaining functional people; however, the reporting relationships shift like the desert sands. It appears that few people assigned to these teams know who they are working for. Instead of two masters there may be several or none at all.

When addressing the management problem posed by these differing requirements of functionality and focus, some time-worn principles can point to a solution. The most applicable are: "One person, one boss," "Responsibility always must be commensurate with authority," "People feel the strongest loyalty to the smallest group with which they identify," and "A focused mind is the most productive." These can be used as guides in achieving something better than is offered by segregated functionality. Where these principles are violated, there is likely to be trouble. It is a good bet that whoever looks at a troubled organization will find some violations of these principles.

PPorP Organizations

In the following discussion, the terms *project*, *program*, and *product* are used rather liberally. Project and program are normally used to describe a coherent activity leading to a desired output. Project is generally thought to be smaller and less complex than a program. Product means exactly that. In each case, something is being created by a group of folks who deserve straightforward and cohesive management. There is little difference in the management requirements for a program, project, or product.

An organization combining the most useful features of a functional structure with the focus to efficiently manage a project, program, or product will have all the people and facilities working toward this single objective under the ultimate direction of a single authority. For brevity and convenience, the following discussions refer to these cohesive, objective-oriented organizations as *PPorP* (Product, Project, or Program) structures. A PPorP organization can take many forms, but should never use or need dotted line relationships, ad hoc teams, committee management, or anything of the like. As we see later in the book, some functions common to two or more PPorP groups may be separate, if management makes a conscious decision to do so to assess the risks versus the rewards.

I strongly believe in the superiority of PPorP organizations over the ever-popular functional ones. I have managed both. I found my job to be much easier when directing a PPorP organization. Better information was available, leading to better decisions. I had control over most of the functions that I needed to define, market, and produce a product. As a functional executive, I spent too much time dealing with organizational squabbles among marketing, sales, manufacturing, and engineering groups. It was common for the marketing or sales director to blame the engineers for product cost, schedule, and design problems, while the engineers blamed the marketing group for inept product definition or unrealistic product schedules. I was dealt with summarily by program/product managers when I was a functional manager. Worse, I was dealt with severely by functional managers when I was a program manager.

Economy of scale is a major driving force behind mergers, acquisitions, and other organizational combinations. With intelligent management, attention efficiencies can be achieved as the company grows and the ratio of fixed costs to sales value goes down (**although risk management is nearly always more uncertain for a large organization than for a small one). As manageable organizations are combined or grow, it is quite easy to allow them to become unmanageable.** All one has to do is to leave the basic organization alone, burdening the management with more and larger reporting entities until a wheel comes off. Further fragmenting a functional structure to reduce control spans is not the answer. Neither is adding layers of managers, which may improve the span of control but further serves to confuse communication links by adding attenuation and garbling information passed between the top and bottom layer. Each added management level reduces the focus on what is really important.

Logic and practice both argue that economies achieved from size can't continue forever as a business grows. Once real product cost improvements begin to be difficult to achieve or market share falls (even though business plans point to a rosy future), it is probably time to consider restructuring the big business into a set of smaller, near autonomous entities.

To reduce structural and control problems, the first step is to simplify existing reporting relationships. A straightforward approach is to model a best (simplest) organization with clear, direct responsibilities and unambiguous reporting, without deciding (for the moment) how to get there. This organization should conform to the responsible executive's perception of the maximum allowable span of control, which is generally considered to be ten or fewer people directly reporting to any manager. Once this organization is laid out, the next step is to define the transition. Where major changes are needed, include the orchestration of an orderly transition over time. Two or more discrete steps and as long as two years may be needed to achieve the desired results. Prudence demands careful review of the effects of each structural change. The form of future change should depend upon the outcome of these reviews.

Some executives may feel that they can't seriously consider a best structure because of unique boundaries that, for them, make such an organization appear unattainable. Even so, it is worthwhile to map out the best that can be had. Upon viewing, it just might look good enough to consider changing the boundaries. The most important gain of these machinations is clear and consistent management direction. **While no organization fixes incompetent management, a PPorP structure with crisp managerial responsibilities makes it relatively easy to identify and deal with managers who consistently fail.**

As we saw, the Stony Mount folks did not seriously consider an orderly shift to a PPorP organization. The Air Force had twisted the arms and minds of Stony Mount top managers, getting them to accept the notion that a matrix organization was the best available under the circumstances. It should have been clear to Stony Mount that the Air Force wasn't likely to jeopardize the Watchdog program by summarily replacing Stony Mount as a major contractor as long as Stony Mount was moving in a direction to satisfy Air Force desires. Had Stony Mount managers really believed in the effectiveness of PPorP structures, they could have immediately transferred as many people as needed to the Watchdog program while diligently providing the proper staffing for their other major programs. Within six months or so, such definite actions would have created a stable environment, except for a few slings and arrows from the Air Force. Even then, Stony Mount executives could have acted as interim program managers until the transition was far enough along to ease the pressure.

Functional groups organized within a PPorP structure work very well as long as the one person, one boss rule isn't violated. It is possible (albeit somewhat difficult) to muck up such a PPorP structure by vague direction from management. Most problems arise when two or more managers think they should be doing the same thing, or conversely, when important jobs fall out between subordinate functional organizations.

Along the way, it is probably worthwhile to comment on some perceived advantages of a purely functional structure when compared to a PPorP one. The arguments most commonly used are these: 1) Professionals and those working in the skilled trades are best organized so there can be close contact with peers and clear career paths, 2) the skills required of functional managers are less diverse than those required of PPorP managers, and 3) functional structures are more stable than PPorP ones; for example, the funding of functional organizations tends to be more stable than for PPorPs since funding dollars are supplied by several programs.

These perceived advantages sound rather good. In fact, they are reasonable arguments for retaining functional groups imbedded in the larger PPorP organizations. However, the principal problem is the lack of focus. **A purely functional organization does not enable managers to properly assess priorities and focus effort on important products, programs, or projects.**

Many professionals do not stay in the field defined by the degrees they earned in school. Few engineering, marketing, or quality organizations employ only graduate engineers, marketing people, or quality specialists. Rather, these organizations employ a multidisciplined staff. **Most people welcome the opportunity to work on a variety of tasks supporting an important objective, particularly when their efforts are unhindered by artificial organizational charters.**

In this day and age, few organizations, even functional ones, stay intact for long. Up, down, and sideways business moves; technological changes; mergers; and product mixes all affect the company structure. Where volatility is endemic, product-centered organizations can minimize change by grouping products, while remembering that **the fewer the organizations, the less conflict for power and resources.**

The funding argument for retaining purely functional organizations is mostly artificial. Management must understand the costs associated with their principal products, projects, or programs. This cost information is corrupted by a functional structure. If a functional group's project, program, or product pieces exceed the funds available to produce them, others will have to subsidize those pieces, no matter how the finance department tries to sort it out. **The very act of trying to realize the advantage of stable functional organizations tends to create a false financial picture, much to the future sorrow of the responsible executive.** In a PPorP organization, the manager incurs and controls the costs. These are much more likely to represent the real costs of the product, project, or program.

We shall now outline the steps for achieving a PPorP organization. The goal is to suggest a process leading to the formation of this structure with a minimum of fuss. The example used is centered about an electronics design and manufacturing company, MAC-TEC Electronics, Inc. (Appendix 1 provides more detail about the MAC-TEC realignment process and a discussion of some of the reasoning of the MAC-TEC management along the way.)

While the example is based on an electronics business, the same considerations can be made for metal fabrication, oil refining, or textile and automotive manufacturing. In fact, by changing organizational names and functions, **the PPorP structure can be applied to almost any useful endeavor.** To be sure, the structure is not always applied to the same degree of effectiveness, but it can be to the advantage of almost everyone when contrasted with a functional structure using matrix overlays.

MAC-TEC Electronics has been a functional organization for some time now, even though the company serves three different markets. One part of MAC-TEC designs and produces specialty integrated circuit devices for the commercial market. Another provides design and systems engineering services worldwide. It has just been awarded a major contract to design, develop, and field an air traffic control system, which will significantly increase the potential sales of this part of the company. The third part produces and markets completed circuit boards, systems, and subsystems for consumer computer products. These products incorporate many of the integrated circuits produced by the device segment of MAC-TEC. The present organization is shown in Figure 2-1.

The following groups fall under the aegis of the engineering department: research and development, systems engineering, device and systems product design, computer-aided design, test equipment design, and document control.

Finance keeps the books, analyzes financial data, performs audits, and monitors planning exercises.

Manufacturing functions include material preparation, production control, production, shipping, and manufacturing engineering (whose tasks are similar to those of industrial engineering, design engineering, and test engineering).

Quality performs specification reviews and certification, product inspections, tests, and factory data collection and analyses. The manufacturing, engineering, and logistics groups also perform pieces of these functions.

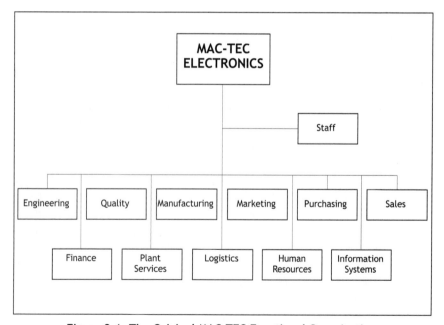

Figure 2-1. The Original MAC-TEC Functional Organization

Plant Services conducts preliminary designs for new construction and fixed equipment and together with the purchasing department, administers the associated contracts. Security, janitorial services, and plant maintenance are all part of the plant services group.

Purchasing (Material Procurement) buys everything the company needs, save a few special items bought directly by local management. This group also maintains inventory records for non-productive items and administers contracts with vendors.

Marketing is responsible for pricing (along with the sales department), general product specifications (sort of), and market definition. Both the sales and marketing groups deal with advertising.

Sales works with distributors and sales representatives, and manages a pair of regional sales offices.

Information Systems is an internal computer systems specifier, procurer, and administrative catchall.

Logistics handles field service, product warranties (defined by the marketing and engineering groups), product repair (except for the specifications), and sales of spares (along with the marketing and sales groups).

Human Resources (Personnel), at the direction of management, hires, fires, trains, disciplines, and administers contracts with the bargaining units.

Staff presently consists of a lawyer, two administrators, three planners, four technical advisors, five ex-vice presidents, six program/project/ product managers with varying responsibilities and little authority, the ex-general manager's old drinking buddy, and a partridge in a pear tree.

Some of the more obvious troublesome sources of conflict among the functions are as follows:

Engineering vs. Quality vs. Manufacturing (Design engineering vs. manufacturing engineering, test equipment design vs. test conduct, and engi-

DILBERT reprinted by permission of United Features Syndicate, Inc.

neering reasonableness checking vs. quality validation of product test specifications).

Engineering vs. Marketing (product definition vs. product specifications and design schedules vs. scheduled product introductions).

Quality vs. Manufacturing (in-process monitoring vs. testing and yield reporting and in-process monitoring vs. quality data collections).

Engineering vs. Manufacturing vs. Finance vs. Information Systems (computer usage management and computer systems specification and selection).

Logistics vs. Sales vs. Quality vs. Marketing vs. Purchasing vs. Engineering (warranty and warranty repair, spares definition, spares pricing, product packaging, field support, and yield/failure rate data).

Sales vs. Marketing (marketing/sales plans and forecasts, product pricing, competitive analyses, advertising, and customer service).

The staff vs. everyone else (staff includes the present program/project/product management).

Anyone who has spent time in a functional organization can undoubtedly add copiously to this list. Incomplete though the list may be, it gives an idea of the state of affairs in a fairly typical functional structure. Even though functional organizations look quite clean on paper, some pretty murky situations lie just beneath the surface.

Figure 2-2 depicts the desired top-level structure of the new MAC-TEC. It so happened that this best organization was not directly achievable. For at least a time, management settled for the organization shown in Figure 2-3.

Figure 2-3 represents a good compromise solution and is a major step toward a full PPorP structure. If it works well in its present form, it may not change for some time. If the systems groups grow sufficiently, Systems Manufacturing may later be separated, with each part reporting to a different systems executive. It will probably be later, rather than sooner, when Central Operations is broken up.

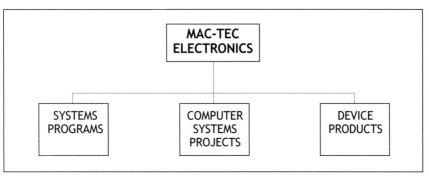

Figure 2-2. Top Level New MAC-TEC Organization (PPorP Structured)

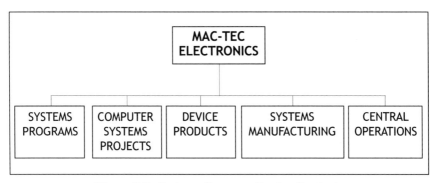

Figure 2-3. Systems Programs Device Products
Top-level Compromise (Possibly Interim) MAC-TEC Structure

The hard part of putting a PPorP organization together is deciding what to do with those functions that don't split out easily. A look at some cases in point may help.

Manufacturing

MAC-TEC Electronics designs and produces integrated circuit (ICs) devices (processors, memories, and the like), completed circuit boards, and complex electronic systems. While systems production and assembly equipment is quite different from that used to produce devices, both manufacturing areas test several end products with similar test equipment using different fixtures and adapters.

A modern electronic systems assembly line typically uses rather sophisticated pick-and-place equipment to put the various electronic parts on printed circuit boards. In well-run factories, all parts to be assembled are tested prior to assembly. These assembled components are then mass-attached to the circuit board, and the board assembly is tested for compliance with the circuit specifications. If the system includes an enclosure, the system electronics board(s) are assembled into the enclosure and tested once again.

An IC wafer line is capital-intensive, requiring extremely expensive equipment to pattern, implant, etch, metalize (test and coat), and saw large silicon wafers. Hundreds (often thousands) of dice on the wafer are tested individually by probing contact points on each die. The wafer is then cut up with the bad die marked with an inkblot. The good dice are selected, bonded, and packaged into finished useful parts, and then tested. Wafer lines usually have several part numbers in work simultaneously, supporting several different projects or customers. Conflicts about the finished product are quite common, making the assignment of production priorities a non-trivial task.

MAC-TEC management decided it would be best to split the manufacturing function into two groups. The systems manufacturing group would report to the CEO, while the device manufacturing group would report to the device products executive. Both manufacturing executives would control their factories lock, stock, barrel, and testers.

A consequence of the split is that the reporting relationship of the device manufacturing group is one notch lower in the organization than that of the systems manufacturing group. This should not in itself affect the relative pay or the decision-making ability of the two executives. **The common view that the higher the reporting level, the more important the job is not necessarily true.** Both manufacturing jobs are of equal importance. The organizational placement was one that best served the company, and it had nothing to do with the merits of the people involved.

At MAC-TEC the two systems businesses, at least for now, deal with a single internal manufacturing organization. It is important that each systems executive have the right to use any manufacturing facility. To motivate the systems manufacturing executive and to allow the executives of the computer systems projects and systems programs groups the freedom to negotiate manufacturing prices, the systems manufacturing group was made a profit (not cost) center. At the same time, the device products executive decided that device manufacturing should also be treated as a profit center.

As long as the manufacturing profit center can create products for no more than the fully accounted price quotes, all is well. Sales and profits will flow to the next higher profit center. If manufacturing performance falters and the profit center becomes a loss center, things aren't quite as simple. Remembering that the main reason for creating profit centers was motivation, the MAC-TEC CEO or the responsible PPorP executive can deal with a profitless happening in one of at least two ways.

Perhaps the easiest way to handle small losses is to note the red ink as it occurs, letting the losses flow to MAC-TEC's balance sheet. If the losses grow, they may have a noticeable adverse effect on the incentive pay of all MAC-TEC people, some through no fault of their own. One of the good things about establishing the manufacturing profit center was that it made each manufacturing organization as autonomous as possible. If a failing in the manufacturing group measurably affects the pay of the manufacturing executive's boss, it is a safe bet that the boss will soon become a de facto manufacturing executive, and that the manufacturing executive will be a pariah.

Another option is to establish a reserve fund controlled by the CEO to cover the odd loss. This fund might be used to make loans to zero out current losses to temporarily troubled profit centers. The loan would be repaid as the profit center regains health. Meanwhile, any incentive pay for people in that center would be correspondingly reduced according to a predetermined and published formula. PPorP executives could also create their own reserves to smooth over valleys if the business profits permitted it, and if they so chose.

The treatment of cost of capital may be an issue, heightened now with increasing attention on the EVA (economic value added) measurement. It is suggested that the cost of all manufacturing capital items be fully charged to the manufacturing profit center. Otherwise, this equipment may appear as if it is free to manufacturing, even though it isn't. The manufacturing executive may then be tempted to try to acquire new capital equipment willy-nilly, using dollars that could be better applied elsewhere.

Both MAC-TEC manufacturing organizations must now be competitive with similar manufacturing operations outside of the company. The three business executives will certainly take their production work to outside facilities if quality, price, and schedule are better than those offered at MAC-TEC. Conversely, both manufacturing arms should have the right to no-bid internal products that require massive infusions of capital, or are not compatible with factory skills or with the existing product mix. In addition to creating a cleaner organization, MAC-TEC management can now get hard data concerning the competitiveness of each of the two manufacturing facilities. Where manufacturing departments are captive cost centers, this information is simply not readily available.

As time passes, manufacturing management will likely have reviewed competing designs, and be in a good position to provide rationality checks on the manufacturability of MAC-TEC engineering designs. The manufacturing group can also help by bidding on production and assembly work from selected outside customers whenever it makes good sense to do so.

Finance

Finance and accounting are usually central functions, often with financial representatives assigned to various products and organizations. Advantages of this lumped financial structure over a distributed one are reported as allowing efficient use of personnel and equipment, better ability to cross-train financial specialists, and providing a central check guarding against financial hanky-panky in the subordinate organizations. The cross-training argument has merit, but the others are flawed. In particular, the hanky-panky checks don't always work as intended.

The Creative Vice President

This crafty man was a vice president and general manager of a moderately sized division that built hybrid microcircuits. He took pride in personally running the division with an iron hand. He didn't appear dishonest, but chicanery turned out to be one of his major strengths.

The parent company's financial organization was centrally managed. It was well-known that the division controllers had two bosses. First and foremost, these controllers reported to the corporate financial executive, with division management running a distant second. Financial representatives (monitors) were assigned to work with each division as financial staff, but they were ready to report back to the central finance office about any problems they found. With these controls in place, company management felt quite comfortable about financial integrity and made the financial performance of each division a major determining factor in computing the incentive compensation paid to executives, including the hybrid vice president.

Hybrid microelectronics are dense, expensive, and incorporate the most difficult electronic assembly techniques. Hybrids should be used only where nothing else will do, and perhaps not then. It is common to miss hybrid schedules and yields by a country mile. These folks generally missed both, making financial performance of the division questionable at best. Since the basic problem wasn't easily fixed, the vice president decided to fix the financial reporting instead. He terrorized the assigned financial employees until they wanted no part of him or his division. They worked at staying out of his way. He and a select few of his confidants began to cook the books. They created sales and profits out of whole cloth. First a little, then more, and eventually creative accounting went into full swing. He altered the month-end and quarterly reports, making the financial performance of the division look good, at least for a hybrid microelectronics group. He did this by reporting as sales, imagined deliveries of hybrid products to internal customers when the hybrids had not yet been completed, let alone delivered. He directed several of the managers in the division to charge work done on fixed-price programs as cost-type contracts.

Most of this chicanery consisted of a Ponzi-like scheme, which by its very nature would be found out in time. So, unless something very positive was in the offing for hybrids, the vice president was sure to be caught. Good rarely happens in the hybrid world. After the best part of a year, a manager at a sister systems division that was supposed to be receiving hybrid largesse and wasn't blew the whistle. Corporate financial folk then noticed that things were not kosher. The whole didn't equal the sum of the parts. The roof fell in on the vice president, and he was sacked. **The fact that there was a central financial organization did not help.**

This vice president's creative work might have been caught earlier if the finance department had been decentralized. Product financial people reporting directly and solely to the business executives tend to be personally concerned with the prompt totting up of inventories and deliveries. These people would undoubtedly have begun to probe the hybrid delivery discrepancies much earlier. As it was, delivered hybrids were typically sent to central warehouses and entered into inventory at the leisure of the central financial folk, often weeks after deliveries had been made. In such an environment, it was virtually impossible to get a current picture of what was going on, so no timely corrective action was taken.

Marketing, Engineering, Sales, et al.

A typical marketing organization probably has more diverse and difficult assignments to delimit than any other, with engineering not far behind.

Attempts to carve out clear responsibilities for marketers generally create unintended conflicts throughout the company. Attempting to resolve these conflicts is much like pulling apart warm taffy. One good way of simplifying the problem is to do as the CEO of MAC-TEC did. He cut off a large piece of marketing and engineering taffy, leaving a few vague interfaces. He created an organization with a broad scope, but with carefully crafted coherent goals. He included in this new group the hard-to-separate activities that plague executives when trying to manage conventional engineering and marketing organizations. He formed this broader discipline by combining most of the marketing, sales, engineering, and logistics/customer service groups. After some thought, he also threw in a dash of finance.

The executive selected to manage such an organization could, of course, come from any of the included disciplines. This person should be a generalist with a good understanding of engineering, the PPorP goals, and the market. While these people don't grow on trees, they are often available within the parent company.

Quality

The proper reporting relationship for the quality department has always been a bone of contention. The platitude that the quality department functions best when functioning independently seems right, but outside of Underwriters Laboratories and a few other places of the same ilk, this department rarely works independently. This function in any industrial entity must report somewhere. The best that is usually done is to have the quality function report to a general manager. In the case of a PPorP structure, this is normally the PPorP executive.

The quality function is frequently placed within other organizations, such as manufacturing/operations. The rationalization is that it improves operating efficiency, but product quality is likely to suffer. Labor costs can be reduced for a time by combining inspection and production functions, making both skills available for fabrication, assembly, and product inspections under the direction of production management. However, this practice often creates a clear conflict of interest. When manufacturing incentives are used, they are dependent on output and yields. It is the unusual individual who opts for a reduction in pay in the interest of preserving quality. With a quality organization independent of manufacturing, marketing, or engineering, specification reviews, analyses, and inspections can be done honestly, with proper feedback, and with a minimum of outside interference.

Service and Central Functions

There are at least four distinct choices for organizing service and central functions in a PPorP structure, with all combinations possible.

1. Direct each PPorP executive to support him or herself with guards, maintenance workers, and so on, splitting up available existing resources among the PPorP organizations. Often there aren't enough people and equipment to go around. Even when there are, managing is often more of a chore than the PPorP business executives wants.

2. Each PPorP group, by mutual agreement, can elect to perform certain services for the others, leaving pieces of the central organizations intact. This doesn't violate any criteria (unless the span of control rules are exceeded), but it does add bother to the already busy PPorP executives. It may also make PPorP executives somewhat less capable of managing their own fate.

3. Another available solution is to leave the central function intact by forming (or reforming) a central organization. If this choice is adopted, create a central profit center that sells services to the PPorP groups in competition with external suppliers. As an added benefit, service organizations can sometimes turn a nice profit. Leaving the central function intact makes the PPorP executive even less a master of his/her own fate, and puts the next higher executive in danger of having to decide janitorial priorities.

4. A fourth choice is to disband the central functions, allowing each PPorP executive to deal with the problem in his or her own way. Generally this option involves taking up the slack internally by the PPorP group and hiring outside contractor support. Often the same contractor can be used by all PPorP functions with the joint approval of the PPorP executives. This is most often the preferred solution, but combinations of any or all of the above can work.

(Additional detail concerning the restructuring of MAC-TEC is in the appendix.)

Transitioning to a PPorP organization can be done to any degree. Steps taken to focus on principal products, programs or projects, while establishing equal responsibility and authority at the lowest possible level, should bear fruit. Whatever the organizational configuration, it is self-defeating to ask anyone to work for more than one boss.

CHAPTER 3

Plan Ahead

"Much may be made of a Scotsman if he be caught young."
- Samuel Johnson

Plans Should Be Managers' Servants, Not Their Masters

GOOD PLANNING HAS ALWAYS BEEN an important managerial goal and one of the bigger managerial failures. We don't seem to handle uncertainties well, and when dealing with the future, there is nothing but uncertainty. Many planning troubles can be attributed to short-term thinking evidenced by statements like, "My bonus depends on the results for this quarter," or "We've got to make this month's sales. Push everything ahead that you can find." People who consistently operate in this hand-to-mouth fashion have a tough time dealing with the future when it becomes the present.

Many of the same executives who stew about monthly business performance demand the preparation of detailed five-year plans. It is the act of planning that seems to satisfy them. Using the planning results to guide the businesses is at best incidental. In my thirty-odd years of experience, **never once did an executive who was responsible for planning call managers together to compare the five-year plans with actual performance or with each other. Such an exercise would have been most instructive.** A major reason these reviews did not take place was that after a few months, the variations between plan and reality were so embarrassing that the plans were relegated to the darkest of archives.

Planning is ever so difficult when done in exquisite, but usually useless, detail. Invariably, planning mistakes involve too much planning rather than too little. Year after year, good managers are required to participate in planning cycles where business plans are constructed over and over again in nauseating detail, becoming obsolete before they are printed.

To make things worse, managers are often required to provide formal business plans tailored to higher management. It is unfortunate that these are often the only plans developed in an orderly way. Typically, these are five-year financial plans called long-range plans, strategic business plans, or something similar. They are usually supported by an annual operating plan, which despite the name, often covers at least two years.

Such plans are rarely believed by perceptive management and, consequently, are seldom used. **Glowing detail does *not* make a plan accurate and real. Meticulous detail is useful only when there are stable and well-understood situations.** To believe any plan exactly represents the future implies short-term thinking and probably bad planning. Those who think that the future can be seen with the clarity of the present aren't thinking too clearly.

A few management theorists teach the principle that the best planning is no planning. They think manpower is wasted in formal planning cycles. However, some degree of planning is usually needed. Anyone trying to get through life with even modest success had better learn to plan early on if only to avoid stumbling into ditches. Planning is important!

Form Should Follow Function, Not the Other Way Around

At the start of a planning cycle conducted by a medium or large company, the chief financial officer (CFO) typically distributes guidelines for the planning information required. The CFO is not particularly concerned about describing a plan to benefit first-line nonfinancial managers. First-line managers, of course, are the people who really run the company. The CFO is normally looking to satisfy the perceptions of general management. This is the first, but not the greatest, mistake the CFO can make. The bigger mistake is the almost universal confusion about precision and accuracy. Even senior managers feel that the more detail provided, the better the description of the subject, no matter whether or not the seminal data is shaky. For any five-year plan, the data affecting the out-years is shaky beyond belief. This overplanning results in plans that contain copious but highly questionable details, generated by the expenditure of millions of managerial and other professional hours each year.

Some businesses are easier to forecast than others, but it is only the odd business activity that can be accurately forecast in any kind of useful detail for more than a couple of years. Five-year forecasts of other than general trends are triumphs of hope over reality, even in so-called commodity businesses. If any real use could be made of these forecasts in the third to the fifth years, the business activity would likely be so stable that such a plan would take on considerably less importance than it is usually given. Possibly morticians enjoy such a predictable business, but even they are subject to business fluctuations from plagues, wars, epidemics, and the occasional attack of wellness.

An interesting example of poor planning happened several years ago when one of the organizations reporting to me was providing programming support to the long range-planners. The long-range planners had been working continuously for years to put together a five-year plan. Each time the current business changed because of the addition of new customers, the loss of old ones, or the product mix changed, the planners started over on major pieces of the plan. As it turned out, they were never able to put together a coherent and complete plan in the several years I was associated with them. During that time, most of our working managers would have been quite pleased to see a useful general plan covering the next six months. Undaunted, the long-range planners were continually authorizing emergency overtime for the creation and modification of computer programs to support all of the unplanned activities and unplanned changes that were an integral part of the long-range planners planning.

After the CFO sets the guidelines, the formal plan normally begins with a sales and marketing forecast of existing products and services. New products and services are then added. Anticipated costs of sales for the next five years are generated to the penny. **These costs will usually underestimate the real cost of putting a product into production and fail to take into account the advantages of production learning curves for both new and existing products.** It will be assumed that the competition will have overpriced its wares so that forecasted product margins are comfortable ones. Forecasted market share is the biggest guess of all. It is often a reflection of what the marketing executive thinks the general manager wants, expressed to the nearest tenth of one percent.

As an example, the following table presents a partial spreadsheet containing the skeleton of an early consortium's five-year plan. The content of this plan has been approved by the consul-treasurer of Titus/Crassus Imports and Manufacturing Ltd. of Ostia for the years of 51 through 55 A.D. The table is but a small sample of planning overkill through the centuries.

Fifty ox carts carried the full completed and unread plan to the ancient archives to languish there with some sixty others until recently unearthed. Note the detail. If anyone believes that the realized sales of erotic ceramics were exactly as planned in LIV A.D., I have for that person a bireme for sale or lease at unbelievable savings. Not to put too fine a point on it, the information in the above table represents an attempt to quantify a set of guesses to an unwarranted level of detail. The same mistake is repeated day after day in the modern world.

Product Development Plans

A sample plan for the development and marketing of a new semiconductor memory device is offered as one example of reasonable and useful plan-

FIVE YEAR PLAN—TITUS/CRASSUS IMPORTS AND MANUFACTURING YEARS LI THROUGH LV

PRODUCTS AND SERVICES PRICES IN DENARII	YEAR LIV (Q1) LOT VOLUME SALES PRICE (LOTS)			YEAR LIV (Q2) LOT VOLUME SALES PRICE (LOTS)			V YEAR TOTAL VOLUME SALES (LOTS)	
RED-FIGURE AMPHORAE (XX PIECE LOTS)	CC	MCIV	CCXXCCM	CL	MCCMV	CCLXXDCCL	XXVMIX	MMMCMCLI
DINING COUCHES (X PIECE LOTS)	CCM	CI	XXCCCM	CMV	CXX	CMMXDC	MMDII	MMCCLXMVCX
EROTIC CERAMICS (C PIECE LOTS)	DCC	MIV	DCCMMCCM	DCXX	MC	DCXXCMM	XLMMC	XMMMDCXLV
TESSARAE (C WEIGHT LOTS)	C	MMM	CCC	CX	MMMC	CCCXLM	LXMVC	MMMXCCLXII
EGYPTIAN OBELISKS (M WEIGHT LOTS)	MCMX	XX	XXXMMXCC	MMX	XX	XLCC	CDXX	MMXCCXLI
BRONZE STATUES LIFE SIZE (II PER LOT)	CD	CLI	LXCD	CDX	CL	LXMD	MMMCCX	MCCXLI
RENTAL OF GREEK MERCENARIES (LOTS OF C MAN-MONTHS)	MVI	DX	DXMMMLX	MVI	DX	DXMMMLX	MVXI	XCVDCXI

TOTAL SALES -DENARII-
XXXMXCDXMXCLXXI

The overline is used here to implicitly multiply the overlined numeral by 1,000; i.e.: V= 5,000. This notation may or may not have been used by the ancient Romans, having been first observed in medieval writings. The double overline indicates that the symbol should be multiplied by another thousand for a multiplier of one million. The double overline may not have been used anywhere else, but it made things neater here.

ning. The ideas presented are evolutionary, not revolutionary, but should be useful for guiding any development planning process.

Future sales of computers, electronics, and software are among the most difficult products to forecast. These businesses are strongly driven by technological advances, which are often breakthroughs and are therefore unseen before they occur. To make matters worse, the products of these businesses are big eaters of capital resources. It takes money and time to build production facilities and to procure needed expensive fabrication equipment. If the product is found to be flawed, to be unpopular, or is beaten to the marketplace by a competitor, most of that front-end money will have been for naught. To get a handle on some of the risks and alternatives, it is an excellent idea to include as an integral part of any development plan answers to questions like, "How different are our planned new products from what others have to offer? How many of these new products are we likely to sell? By when? How long are our old products going to continue to sell when the new products hit the marketplace?" As for breakthroughs, it is impossible to plan for things one doesn't know about. Not to worry, intelligent planning to guide future actions is still possible. It requires some thought, a look to the past, and a few decisions tempered by a reasonableness check or two.

A Method to Our Madness

A time-phased plan is essential for each major new product before much money is spent pursuing the idea. This initial plan should contain enough detail to provide the responsible executive with sufficient information either to authorize or reject the project. It should be of a form that permits easy addition of cogent information and modification. Such a plan might include the following information:

- A brief description of the product and of competing products.

- Who will likely buy the proposed product and when?

- What competition is likely to be faced? Does the new product compete with our existing products?

- Estimated resources needed to do the job including engineering, marketing, manufacturing, and quality costs expressed in dollars, personnel, equipment, and facilities. The most useful time frame for the basic plan should be from the present to one year in the future. A second year or portion thereof would add to the plan utility if there is sufficient substance to warrant it. Also essential to include is a qualitative assessment of the risks involved in bringing the new product to market, and a recognition of anything unique that might be necessary to design, develop, market, and produce it.

• Estimated measure of product profit or loss.

• At the end, a small space should be reserved for the responsible executive to approve or disapprove the proposed development. **The executive should not be allowed to equivocate. Accept or reject should be the only options.**

If the project is accepted, the plan should be reviewed, modified when necessary, and validated. The updated, signed-off plan should be in the hands of working management by the time work is started. Usually a number of unexpected things appear once the people involved realize they are going to have to work on something real instead of something planned. **Updating is nearly always needed and is the second phase of the sequential plan.** Once the plan is updated, the responsible executive should conduct a brief review with the boss to discuss the essentials. **While minor changes from the original plan are to be expected and will likely result in increased costs, anything major at this point is indicative of uncertain planning or wishful thinking, making the entire project suspect.**

If the validation hurdle is successfully passed, the project can now be thought of as real and serious implementation can begin. Many plans fail at the outset. **Without firm early guidance, resources tend to be initially applied in a desultory fashion.**

Plan updates should be made only when the product executive feels it to be necessary, not when financial management wants it. Reviews should be conducted at least quarterly, more often when surprises surface. The presumption should be that the plan is always current and valid. There will then never be less than nine months worth of good planning to continually guide the business. You can add more detail to the plan, but further detail should be presented in the form of actual data.

Failure to update the plan when first needed should affect the responsible executive's pay.

With the existence of a current plan for each project, the need for the yearly sterile and resource-consuming planning exercises is minimal. Costs and margins for all products, projects, and programs—the lion's share of the business—should be a matter of adding the product plans together.

When significant discontinuities occur between actuals-to-date and future plans, management should find out the reasons. Significant deviations are generally on the order of 10-20% of costs or margins, but different managers will likely have different thresholds. Managers should quickly examine surprises, treating them as early warning triggers assessing the worth of the active plans even if financial performance is on track.

Risks should be identified only so they can be minimized or avoided. Risk assessment should be an honest look at stumbling blocks and possible financial downers that can, with reasonable probability, be associated with new product development and sales. Risk assessment should not be the beginning of a Pearl Harbor file.

THE PLAN

As you may recall from an earlier discussion, MAC-TEC Electronics was recently recast from a functional to a product-centered organization. Although good planning is not dependent on organizational structure, it is easier and more meaningful in a product-centered, rather than functional, organization. **Even more essential to good planning are good managers and good planners working with good information.**

During the MAC-TEC restructuring, memory products were integrated into the device products group along with several other integrated circuit products. All necessary skills and facilities were made available under a single leader to conceive, specify, design, and produce this new product.

Armed with ideas for the new memory design, the device product developers talked with system houses to see if they needed the memory widget they were considering. Customers were interested, but each wanted something a little different than the next, and different from the original product design. Following the discussions, the original conceptual design was changed to accommodate several of the customer desires.

MEMORY PRODUCTS
MULTI-MEGABYTE MEMORY DEVELOPMENT AND SALES PLAN

PRODUCT DESCRIPTION

A multi-megabyte tri-port memory will be designed and produced in the CMOS 2000 process. This part will be designed to be expanded as production technology permits higher densities. The initial die size will be approximately 144 square mm. The speed, specialty logic, package detail and pinouts can be found in engineering report 1-234. Projected yields are 100 die per wafer initially, increasing substantially linearly with wafer starts to 850 die per wafer at maturity.

PRODUCT MARKET

The design of this part has been coordinated with, and approved by Micro Video, Rising Sun Displays, and Maple Leaf Computing, Inc. All are in the process of designing systems using this part. Customer samples are required by October 2001, with initial production quantities January 2002. An alternate source will be licensed by June 2001.

COMPETITION

No comparable part exists. Sales of the Multi-Megabyte Memory will have no impact on the planned sales of our other devices. Competition will likely begin copying as soon as samples are delivered. Competing sample parts from either (or both) Shifting Sands Semiconductor and Microwafers Ltd. are expected to be offered for sale about one year after our first customers receive the samples.

DESIGN ASSETS REQUIRED

The design team will consist of one senior design engineer, one circuit designer (half time), one logic designer (quarter time), one layout designer, and one test engineer as needed. All are presently available for the project start. One layout station will be devoted full time to this project. No modification of circuit analysis or layout programs is anticipated. Part-unique probe/package test programs and fixtures will be developed. No other special equipment is anticipated. Documentation will consist of engineering drawings upgraded for external release, a product flier, a detailed product description, and a test specification.

PRODUCTION COSTS

MAC-TEC Device Manufacturing developed costs. These will be confirmed at the completion of the manufacturing review of the final design. Alternate source bids are expected at the same time. The mix of production quantities (internal vs. external) will be decided then.

RISKS

Known risks include the possibility that one or more of our potential customers will drop or delay development plans for the systems using our part, or will find an acceptable substitute. Continuous contact with the customers' design engineers is essential for early warning and to insure that they have our support. If the Multi-Megabyte Memory samples are more than two months late, the risk of being dropped by one or more of our potential customers becomes near-certainty. Other product risks are judged no higher than the normal risk of doing business

Once the preliminary detailed design was validated to a level of detail including things like device functions, pin-outs, die size, and test requirements, the design team could then put the development and sales plan together.

The financial portion of the development plan is shown as a spreadsheet, but unlike similar plans, it provides for the inclusion of actual data when generated. This makes plan/actual comparisons easy and obvious. The plan is limited to a two-year period.

The **product line costs** should include all costs incurred by people reporting to the device products group. This includes managers, design engineers, computer engineers, test engineers, marketers, sales staff, financial specialists, quality monitors, and technical writers. These costs include occupancy costs, depreciation, fringe benefits, and the like.

The **fixed price support** in this example is entirely from the MAC-TEC device manufacturing group. Even though manufacturing is integrated with the device products group, it is considered a profit center. The manufacturing fixed-price bid is treated as a price. Note that the price associated with the manufacturing effort is used by the planners as both planned and actual costs. These costs will be accumulated as time passes. Any additional work requested from the manufacturing group as the product matures will be rebid and negotiated in the same way as the original bid. Some suggested methods of handling inevitable fixed price versus cost variations are discussed in Chapter 2.

Required capital is seen as both planned and actual expenditures. MAC-TEC reports capital outlays as actual costs when the funds are committed.

Total costs are the quarterly accumulation of all relevant product costs, summarized yearly.

Sales are reported in delivered units and as sales value. Both are important. Units delivered are used by management as an aid for assessing manufacturing production capacities and rates for all products. In the MAC-TEC plan, the planned unit rates were validated contingent upon the timely delivery of firm design information to the manufacturing group.

MULTI-MEGABYTE MEMORY
DEVELOPMENT COSTS AND SALES DATA (EXPRESSED IN THOUSANDS OF DOLLARS)

	FY00					FY01				
	Q1	Q2	Q3	Q4	TOTAL	Q1	Q2	Q3	4	TOTAL
PRODUCT LINE COSTS										
PLANNED	80	90	100	60	330	50	50	50	50	200
ACTUAL	32	81	113	97	323	—	—	—	—	—
DEVIATION	48	9	(13)	(37)	7	—	—	—	—	—
FIXED PRICE SUPPORT										
(MANUFACTURING)	10	10	20	50	90	40	65	150	150	405
REQUIRED CAPITAL										
PLANNED	10				10	100				100
ACTUAL	15	11	—	—	26	—	—	—	—	—
DEVIATION	(5)	(11)	—	—	(16)	—	—	—	—	—
TOTAL COSTS										
PLANNED	100	100	120	110	430	190	115	200	200	705
ACTUAL	57	102	133	147	439	—	—	—	—	—
DEVIATION	43	(2)	(13)	(37)	(9)	—	—	—	—	—
SALES (UNITS)										
PLANNED	—	—	—	100	100	600	1600	5000	15000	22200
ACTUAL	—	—	—	50	50	—	—	—	—	—
DEVIATION	—	—	—	(50)	(50)	—	—	—	—	—
SALES VALUE										
PLANNED				10	10	60	130	400	1100	1690
ACTUAL	—	—	—	5	5	—	—	—	—	—
DEVIATION	—	—	—	(5)	(5)	—	—	—	—	—
PRODUCT MARGIN										
PLANNED	(100)	(100)	(120)	(100)	(420)	(130)	15	200	900	955
ACTUAL	(57)	(102)	(133)	(142)	(434)	—	—	—	—	—
DEVIATION	43	(2)	(13)	(42)	(14)	—	—	—	—	—

PREPARED BY _____, PRODUCT LINE MANAGER

_____ APPROVED _____ DISAPPROVED

(The manufacturing group controls, and is entirely responsible for, the timed flow of parts through the factory to meet the agreed dates.)

Product margin is taken here as product sales income, minus all product costs. Revenue is calculated quarterly and summarized yearly. Any question of timing between funds committed, funds paid, invoices sent, and payment received can best be resolved by the accountants, but it must not obscure the true margin by reporting delays or by odd time-phasing of the elements. **This is a control system. Delays in receiving or acting upon information adversely affect the stability of the system.**

Cash Flow is always a bit tricky to report, involving an accumulation of income received and dollars paid out to date on the Multi-Megabyte Memory program. Some managers like to estimate cash flow as the time accumulation of product margin, set over one billing cycle. If bills are paid on time and receivables flow rapidly, the differences between integrated margin and cash flow may be constant and predictable. Tracking both margin and cash flow here was thought to be a little redundant.

The plan data can be presented and accumulated at more frequent intervals as long as managers recognize that more frequent reporting expends valuable resources, which could lead to shorter-term thinking. This in turn may give rise to unnecessary plan changes and fruitless searches in an attempt to determine causes of normal variations from the plan.

MULTI-MEGABYTE MEMORY
DEVELOPMENT COSTS AND SALES DATA (EXPRESSED IN THOUSANDS OF DOLLARS)

CASH FLOW	FY00				FY01			
	Q1	Q2	Q3	Q4	Q1	Q2	Q3	Q4
PLANNED	(0)	(100)	(200)	(320)	(420)	(510)	(355)	50
ACTUAL	(20)	(120)	(212)	(308)	—	—	—	—
DEVIATION	(20)	(20)	(12)	12	—	—	—	—

Planning, Structure, and Form

Most organizations have some people working on tasks not directly accountable to a project. There were some ancillary MAC-TEC costs not included in this simple sample plan. These included costs that were generated by general management, trial lawyers, environmental cleanup, a consultant, a few facilities improvements, and institutional advertising. These were, for the most part, not under the control of the product executive. They represent a small tax on the product and are best accumulated by MAC-TEC as a whole, not by the device products groups. These costs should be recognized in the MAC-TEC summary plan and one-year-forecast. For a true product-organized company, that's all there is to it.

Note, too, that a good measure of any product line's contribution to the organization's sales and profit can now be had without allocating central costs to the products (except for the few above-noted tasks). **No clear thinker will try to plan for a third year.**

Where the organization isn't structured by product, program, or project, additional complexities will likely be present. Management may feel the need to separate product costs into direct charges and indirect charges (also referred to as burden charges). For PPorP structures, all required expenditures can be considered direct charges, despite some financial doctrine to the contrary. The development plan should not support any artificial application of costs by simply distributing central costs to the output unless there is a traceable and rational allocation scheme. Even then, these central costs should always be obvious and shown all together to top management.

The original plan should be used for at least a year and compared with real data. The more public the exposure, the better.

The Big Parade

Good planning isn't easy. Even in simple cases, people may presume or simply won't ask the right questions. What follows is a true story about a strong desire to plan and order the future and a failure to do so.

From the 1947 East High School yearbook.

East High School ROTC Platoon

The place was East High School in Salt Lake City, Utah. It was springtime. The weather was warm and breezy, with a few cotton clouds overhead. The day began for the cadet ROTC officers with a 6:30 a.m., before-school meeting. They were there to listen carefully to the Professor of Military Science and Tactics (PMS&T) give his orders for the smooth execution of the big flag lowering parade to take place on Army Day. The new PMS&T had dropped in from nowhere a few weeks before. The new man was a first lieutenant, a paratrooper, complete with razor sharp creases in his bloused pantaloons tucked into brilliantly polished paratrooper boots. He clearly expected all of the budding child officers in the East High ROTC battalion to be as eager as he was. Some were. Most weren't.

The cadet officers met that morning in the smelly yellow calcimined muster room on the bottom floor of the school near the gym. Lt. Black began his motivational lecture by charging the cadet officers to safeguard the collective honors of the president of the United States; the newly created Defense Department; the U.S. Army; and all paratroopers, past, present, and future. Lt. Black ordered each cadet officer to insure that there would be no foul-ups during the planned flag lowering ceremony by religiously following the detailed plan he had personally developed. His preparations were meticulous. The parade route was laid out with care. The band rehearsed, rehearsed, and then rehearsed some more. For each practice parade, the battalion's Enfield rifles were cleaned, inspected and re-cleaned. Uniforms were examined for spots and creases. Shoes were spit-shined. Each company was drilled over the planned parade route until tracks were worn in the grass.

Lt. Black considered the student body and faculty unimportant distractions. They were mere civilians that he would allow to be spectators. The real audience was a man who sat at the right hand of God, a regular army major who would review the troops. Lt. Black knew this was to be one of the most important days of his life, and he would leave *no stone unturned* to insure a ceremony that would go down in the annals of East High as an example of military precision.

Salt Lake City Schools always lacked funds. At that time, they were so poor that the eighth grade was eliminated. The excuse was that everything normally taught in the seventh and eighth grades could be taught in one year. This carried the venerable 80/20 rule to the extreme. That is to say, **80 percent of the useful information imparted in most classes and management seminars can be put across in about 20 percent of the time.** However, the belief that one can get across one 100 percent of the information in 50 percent of the time is highly suspect. When this grade elimination didn't allow them to meet the budget, the board authorized doubled-up instruction in language classes. The afternoon of the parade, two Latin classes scheduled at the same hour had but one instructor. She would be in each class for half the period, leaving the students unsupervised the other half. For one of the cadets, this seemed to be an ideal opportunity to test Lt. Black's dictum that he would leave no stone unturned.

It is safe to say that the most important single thing at the beginning of a flag lowering ceremony is a billowing flag at the top of the flagpole. Any thinking individual planning a successful flag ceremony would certainly check that a flag was flying, wouldn't he?

The young cadet solemnly marched from his Latin class to the flagpole at the front of the school. He unwound the lanyard and slowly and respectfully lowered the flag in full view of the principal's office and about 30 classrooms. He then folded the flag in the prescribed manner, once lengthwise, followed by triangular folds with the blue field folded last. He put the flag under his arm, marched through the large oak double doors, and put Old Glory away in the closet where it was normally kept. Several people saw him, but no one noticed. Acting as though all was legitimate was excellent cover. The whole process took perhaps five or six minutes. When the bell rang signifying an end to the sixth period, the ROTC cadets formed on the football field. The students who could escape the campus did so unnoticed. The rest were shepherded to the front of the building and faced toward the flagpole to witness the ceremony.

The cadets didn't get to see too many high-ranking Army officers. In spite of the major's exalted rank, he looked pretty normal. He seemed a little overweight, wore glasses, had thinning hair, and smiled a little. Lt. Black escorted the major to his rightful place of honor atop the front steps of the school. The principal, and those of the faculty who couldn't get away, were assigned spots so that they did not interfere with the major's view. The principal was placed two paces behind and one pace to the left of the major.

Once order was established and the major was standing comfortably, Lt. Black gave the command for the battalion to proceed. The cadet battalion commander gave his order. The company commanders gave each of their orders. "Right Face...Right Shoulder Arms...Forward March!" The band began to play the *National Emblem March*, unfortunately not all at once, but after a few steps they were all playing with enthusiasm.

It took some doing to get the battalion around to the front of the school building. During the many practices, the field was clear. No one expected that several visiting cars would be parked in the way of the march, and of course, no one checked. The cadets broke into a rough skirmish line. They did a good job dodging the cars, scraping only one or two with their Enfield rifles.

The battalion finally came to the front of the flagpole, faced right, and waited at attention for the ceremony to begin. None of the approximately 1,500 people present, including Lt. Black, noticed no flag flew. As the band began to play, the color guard snapped to and marched up to the flagpole. The band stopped playing. The lead guard slowly undid the lanyard. The trumpet player readied himself to play *Retreat*. All was still. The young guard looked up expecting to see the flag billowing from the top of the pole. He saw only rope and gasped, "My God! It isn't there." His voice cracked in mid-God, lending an appropriate element to the proceedings.

When Lt. Black noticed the absence of red, white, and blue, he was galvanized into inaction. After an interminable and embarrassing silence, the trumpet player decided to go for *Retreat*. Once he finished, there was a crushing silence. The major finally cleared his throat. The student body shuffled and began to drift off. The principal saved the day by stepping three paces forward turning and saying, "Lieutenant, that was a fine ceremony. I wouldn't concern myself about a little detail like not having a flag. I thought it was all splendid and suggest that you dismiss us now."

Lt. Black looked over to the major, who shook his head slowly and walked to his car. The faculty and the student body rapidly dispersed. The ROTC battalion marched around the back and fell out. The band broke up where they stood. Lt. Black was left seething.

The next day, Lt. Black called the battalion officers together. He demanded to know the name of the person or persons who caused him, the President, The Joint Chiefs, the U.S. Army, and particularly the paratroopers so much embarrassment. Praise be to God, he never found out.

Perhaps this story contains more than one moral, but the intent is to dramatize the notion that **competent and successful managers not only plan to a level of detail commensurate with the task at hand, but continually check to see that the plan is being followed. When something is going (or has gone) awry, they take swift action to correct the problem, and where necessary, revise the plan before the situation becomes a disaster.**

The Planned Loss

The following is the complete text of a Boeing news release airing surprisingly bad financial news for the world's largest commercial aircraft builder.

SEATTLE, Oct. 22, 1997

Boeing to Report Third Quarter Loss

After completing the review of the cost impact of the production recovery plan announced on Oct. 3, 1997, Phil Condit, Boeing chairman and CEO, reported today that Boeing will report a loss for the third quarter of 1997. Condit stated that the production problems being experienced on the commercial aircraft programs reached unexpected levels late in the third quarter. The Company is in the midst of an unprecedented production rate buildup for the 7-series commercial aircraft programs, and has experienced raw material shortages, internal and supplier parts shortages, and productivity inefficiencies associated with adding thousands of new employees. These factors have resulted in significant out-of-sequence work. Condit noted that the breadth and complexity of the entire commercial aircraft production process, especially during this time of substantial production rate increases, present a situation where disrupted process flows are causing major inefficiencies throughout the entire process chain. Under the current recovery plan, the 747 and 737 production lines are being halted for approximately one month. Process inefficiencies and workarounds will continue until the entire process is substantially back in balance, which is expected to occur in 1998. Condit stated that charges associated with these recovery plans and late delivery costs will total approximately $1.6 billion pretax for the third quarter of 1997, and that the continuing recovery plan disruptions will also impact commercial aircraft segment earnings through 1998. Based on a successful execution of the current production recovery plans, it is expected that additional production disruption costs in the range of $1 billion pretax will be incurred over this time period. **A substantial portion of the total third quarter earnings charges result from the unplanned production inefficiencies being experienced on the NextGeneration 737 program.** Based on the production recovery plan, $700 million of the third quarter loss is associated with the initial program accounting quantity of 400 aircraft for the NextGeneration 737 program. Condit noted the cash expenditures associated with the production disruptions and recovery plans will approximate the reduced earnings through 1998. Full third quarter results will be reported on Friday, Oct. 24. **Forward-looking information is subject to risk and uncertainty. Forward-looking statements such as projections of future deliveries, sales, margins, research and development and effective tax rates are subject to risk and uncertainties that could cause actual results to differ materially from those contemplated in the forwardlooking statements.** Among these are the risks and uncertainties identified under the heading 'Forward-looking Information Is Subject to Risk and Uncertainty' accompanying 'Management's Discussion and Analysis of Results of Operation, Financial Condition and Business Environment' in the Boeing 1996 Annual Report to Shareholders and 'Management's Discussion and Analysis of Financial Condition and Results of Operations' in the report on Form 10Q for the second quarter of 1997.

I believe this could have been said somewhat more directly.

SEATTLE, Oct. 22, 1997
We're sorry to have to report the largest quarterly business loss in U.S. history. We got caught up with the thrill of the chase and bit off a lot more than we could chew. We tried to avoid these losses. We planned for everything in exquisite detail. In fact, one reason that things got

away from us is that our managers were tied up planning and replanning each time we made a major acquisition. We made plans, monthly and quarterly, well into the next century. You'd have thought that would been more than enough to keep us out of trouble. Unfortunately, no one paid a lot of attention to these plans because they didn't describe what was really going on.

We coerced our suppliers and subsidiaries into promising virtually impossible schedules, which we dutifully entered into our plans with little thought of the risks. We put too much top management attention on trying to integrate our purchases into our grand scheme. In retrospect it would have been a lot better if we had considered McDonnell Douglas and the North American part of Rockwell International, as wholly-owned profit centers. We should have let their management manage while we concentrated on our airplane business, waiting until we had that back under control before we tried to deal with our acquisitions.

We believed our own press releases that we were darn near invincible, and that we had driven our competition into the ground. Now they are snapping at our heels with renewed vigor, and our customers are worried about our ability to deliver. Unfortunately, their concerns are fully justified. Because our precision planning and reporting processes are so badly time-phased and, hence, inaccurate, we won't know the true extent of the damage for years, if ever. We have forgotten how to manage building airplanes and have shut down our lines until we can bring some order out of the chaos.

We apologize to our stockholders, to our government, and to our airline customers (particularly anyone whose business plans will be severely disrupted because of our failures), but we are not likely to change the planning process we have used for some fifty years. So, in a few years from now, we will probably do it all over again.

Subsequent events continue to show the seriousness of the Boeing problems. As of this writing (spring of 1998), and judging from the later Boeing press releases, the worst may not yet be over. Although the problems should yield to the extraordinary and expensive efforts applied, the Boeing planning processes remain essentially unchanged.

DILBERT reprinted by permission of United Feature Syndicate, Inc.

CHAPTER 4

It's Results That Count

"If I could find out Grant's brand of whiskey,
I would send every general in the field a barrel of it."
– Attributed to Abraham Lincoln

THE COMPLEAT MANAGER MUST BE able to search out and find the triggers that positively motivate human behavior. The manager should map the forest while identifying the bigger trees for later use. It is essential to understand details of the business, but unless one can sort out the trivial issues from the important issues, success will be elusive.

Managers are subjected to continuous and diverse demands. If these demands are acted upon indiscriminately, they lead away from important goals. The important issues can be obscured by day-to-day mundane requests or sidetracked by treating near-trivial problems with the same degree of care that should be applied to serious ones. **It is the excellent executive who can keep the vital separated from the trivial. It is the rare executive who can act quickly, decisively, and correctly on incomplete data.** While not exactly a manager, the lieutenant in our next tale made the right decision, at the right time. Unfortunately, he also paid a price.

No Good Deed Should Ever Go Unpunished

During the Korean War, Americans were very wary of the Soviets attacking our West Coast in force. We feared their capability to destroy our complex of war production facilities, not to mention a large segment of our population. There may have been equal concern about other parts of the country, but this tale is set on the West Coast.

Seattle, San Francisco, and Los Angeles were presumed to be prime West Coast targets. Hamilton Air Force Base, located at San Rafael (more precisely, Novato) in California, was one of several interceptor bases near San Francisco. Hamilton AFB was beautiful. It had eucalyptus trees, lush green lawns, and white Spanish-style buildings located on the shore of the San Pablo Bay, a northern extension of the San Francisco Bay. The main runway ran parallel to the bay shore and was often obscured by fog. Although the fog helped make life cool and pleasant, it did nothing positive for flight safety.

At the time, Northrup F-89 Scorpions were the interceptor aircraft stationed at Hamilton AFB. The F-89s were known affectionately as "Northrup's Follies." They were twin jets, big for the time, weighing more than 40,000 pounds. Their operational range was a little over 1,300 miles, which wasn't far for their assigned intercept missions. It was important that the F-89s had an unobscured landing site when they returned. Among other things, this meant forecasting whether fog would be rolling in at the time a fighter group arrived. Alternate landing fields near Sacramento and at Fairfield-Suisun were available, but if they were to be used, the F-89s time on station would have to be correspondingly reduced. If the aircraft lingered too long, and the fog came just before the F-89s arrived, things could get very sticky for the tired pilots.

The weather station at Hamilton was located in a concrete blockhouse with no windows. This was embarrassing for the duty forecaster when his forecasts for the next hour or so were found to be quite at odds with the weather going on outside. (Even today, there are a number of weather stations throughout the country housed in buildings with no windows.) The forecasting record at Hamilton AFB for predicting fog was not good. It was right only about 50 percent of the time, or what one might achieve

Northrup F-89 Scorpion

by flipping a coin. On the nights fog was forecast, the F-89s would be diverted to another field where the crews would be forced to spend the night. If no fog occurred, the crews would have spent an uncomfortable night away from home for nothing. When good visibility was forecast, fog would roll in about half the time, causing the F-89s to divert quickly to an alternate field or to make a ground-controlled instrument approach to Hamilton in very low visibility conditions. After living with the poor forecast results for well over a year, it was decided to pull the interceptors back early regardless of the meteorological pronouncements.

This state of affairs embarrassed the major commanding the Hamilton weather service detachment. In an attempt to improve matters, he ordered a forecasting contest to begin. The forecaster who could provide the highest percentage of accurate predictions of San Pablo Bay fog would be publicly honored. The forecasting staff hatched new and often complicated theories. Rates of temperature and dew point changes were examined in great detail. The forecasters tried vainly to correlate winds, pressure patterns, and cloud cover with the occurrence of the elusive fog. The success rate did not improve, but help was at hand.

A new lieutenant arrived fresh from weather school. After a brief indoctrination period, the major encouraged him to enter the fog forecasting contest. The major said, "Even though you have little experience, we hope that you have come to us with fresh ideas." Armed with this encouragement, the lieutenant went to work. After a week or so of review and thought, he began making fog forecasts. These forecasts proved to be accurate about 80 to 85% of the time. At first this was taken as beginners' luck. As the summer turned to fall, the lieutenant's accurate forecasts continued unabated. The other forecasters began to believe that he must be doing something right, but the lieutenant wasn't talking.

After six weeks of silent and successful fog forecasting, the major called the lieutenant into his office. After briefly congratulating the lieutenant for his efforts, the major said, "Lieutenant, I want to know how you do it. I have told higher headquarters about this work. It will be a real feather in our cap to show that we have finally solved this vexing problem." The lieutenant demurred saying, "Sir, you may not want to know the details of what I have been doing." The major was not about to be put off. He barked, "This is an order! Tell me about your technique and tell me now!"

The lieutenant shifted about uneasily and said, "Sir, it really is nothing. I examined the history of the fog occurrence here for the past couple of years. I observed that the fog comes and goes in long runs of a week or more. If it comes in today the chances are good that it will come in tomorrow as well. So my forecasts for each day simply involved writing down yesterday's weather. Of course, I missed the forecast when things changed, but this was only once a week or so. I have no idea why it works. I only know that it does."

The major was livid. He roared, "Lieutenant, you've made a travesty out of the science of meteorology. I am embarrassed for all of us. This will go on your record. I will not permit this kind of joke to persist. You will discuss this with no one. Any forecasts you make from now on will be based on conventional and proven techniques. I will tell headquarters that your work was due to luck and cannot be of any value."

The San Pablo Bay fog forecasts were once again wrong about as often as they were right. F-89s were diverted from Hamilton on a regular basis because of the unforecasted fog. All returned to normal. For his inventiveness, the lieutenant was sent to Korea. He might have been sent to Korea anyway.

The poor, but inquisitive, lieutenant had found what the mathematicians and philosophers call a heuristic solution. It is something that is self-learned. We don't always know why it works, we just know that it does. **It is nice, but not essential to know exactly why things happen.** If we think about it for a moment, we find that we really don't know the "why" of much of anything. Why are we here? Why was the universe formed? Who are we, and what are we really made of? Only a few years ago, most of the scientific community believed that Newtonian physics could describe almost everything. Einstein, Bohr, Dirac, Heisenberg, Schrodinger, Hawking, and a host of others have since demonstrated that our knowledge of the true nature of things around us still has some pretty serious gaps. For many people, the now famous experiment demonstrating that a single electron can pass simultaneously through two separate and distinct slits is a bit difficult to swallow. Some recent experimentation suggests that the speed of light may not be the hard limit we have believed it to be. Is nothing sacred?

Since the great minds of the twentieth century have admitted to gaps in their knowledge, it shouldn't bother the rest of us to act on incomplete data. We should be able to feel comfortable when we have an unambiguous, albeit incomplete, basis for our actions as our lieutenant did when forecasting the fog. It would have been nice to have a detailed and valid atmospheric model supporting these forecasts, but failing that, historical data was acceptable. The heuristic method had a major advantage over all other choices at the time. It worked.

Too many managers conduct never-ending searches for yet more information before they act. These quests may be honest ones, or they may be excuses for inaction driven by fear of criticism. This so-called "paralysis by analysis" does no one good. **Trouble occurs for the organization when the boss continually stews over important decisions with no effort to get added useful data and little prospect of finding any.** Mulling over an important pending decision for a day or two may be justified if there is something to think about or there is new cogent information in the offing.

Managers are called upon to make more decisions in the course of a business day than most realize. Fortunately, most of these decisions have less than earthshaking consequences and need minimal time to research and contemplate. Nearly a quarter of the decisions I was asked to make were trivial in nature. It really didn't matter much what my decision was. The important thing was to decide something. Once the decision was made, people had an approved course of action and could move out with authority. **The amount of effort put into deciding a course of action should be strongly related to the reward for getting it right, or conversely, to the penalty for getting it wrong.**

Brochures, briefings, and BS don't substitute for results. An ex-chairman of a large computer firm that used to be much larger, and at this writing is becoming smaller still, follows this personal dictum, "It doesn't make much difference what you do as long as you brief and advertise it all properly." This bit of wisdom comes from a man who was a believer in the ultimate power of publicity. In his speeches and his everyday dealings, he said all of the right words sincerely. He meant none of them. The value of his word diminished in direct proportion to the time one knew him, which is unfortunate. He is a bright fellow, a Ph.D. who early on learned, used, and validated sophisticated techniques to pull the wool over the eyes of his associates and bosses. He could have been an excellent manager or scientist, or even both, but he preferred to walk the easy roadway to success. His star doesn't shine as brightly now, and he has taken a lot of good people down with him. Perhaps now he is closer to believing that the results are what really count.

Good results don't come easy. Even when it seems that things are going swimmingly, it is a good idea to conduct informal checks on the progress and state of things reported by others. People do not intentionally lie, but they often shade things to their benefit, and often they haven't considered the potentially damaging pitfalls. **Problems can occur when completion or near completion of an assignment is reported without having put the results to the test or without finishing the associated required controlling documents.**

"Boss, the computer program is complete. It's on time and within budget."

"Did the program checkout go as you planned?"

"Well, we haven't finished checkout, but we haven't seen any bugs so far."

"Have you run all of the critical and pathological test cases?"

"Not yet, but we've been through better than half of the branches and all of the modules, so probably 90% of the code has been checked."

"How about the manuals and help files?"

"We are going to start on those as soon as we finish checkout."

Instead of being completed, this program may be no more than half-finished in terms of both time and effort!

Shortcuts are fine as long as everyone involved fully understands what they entail and accepts them. They are not good when they are conceived in a near vacuum and their existence is reported in passing at the eleventh hour.

Consider the following discussion between the head of product engineering and the product executive for a new sports car model about to be committed to production.

Head: "I'm proud to report that the product engineering group has made all the necessary drawing and specification changes to reflect the modifications made as a result of the prototype assembly of the Spacefire sports car. We have delivered all required engineering information to the production people early and under budget."

Executive: "That's quite an accomplishment. Normally, the new models have been into production for weeks or months before all of the final paper gets to production. All the drawings are clean? No red lines?"

Head: "Well, there are a few red lines, but it is my understanding that the floor supervisors have agreed to accept them as final."

Executive: "Has the quality group agreed as well?"

Head: "We haven't talked formally with that group, but the quality managers haven't voiced any complaints."

Executive: "Do you know the reasons for the redlined changes?"

Head: "Of course. We found last-minute minor problems with the antilock brake system, the fuel injectors, and the engine mounts."

Executive: "These don't appear to be simple problems. What do you mean by minor?

Head: "In the case of the ABS, we saw a little too much noise on the wheel speed pickoff. The injectors showed a low-level oscillation, and the engine mounts were a little out of tune. Remember, we had to add some weight to the engine a while back. Everything can be fixed easily by simple in-house rework."

Executive: "Are you sure you won't need to replace a purchased part or two? If it turns out that your rework plan isn't sound, we could have a serious line stoppage."

Head: "Have no fear. My people tell me that production can perform all the rework with their eyes closed. In addition, one of our engineers talked to a purchasing agent some time ago. Neither saw a need to stop deliveries of the affected parts or to order replacements. Meanwhile, we will formalize these changes well in time for the next buy cycle."

While it's possible that the initial Spacefire assembly process will withstand these last minute "minor" changes, it is more likely that disaster awaits. Anxious to get production rolling, it appears that Engineering has quietly slipped in some modifications without fully testing them and without proper coordination. Not wanting to create waves and honestly believing the problems to be only minor bugs, the engineers got their modifications accepted informally. A tipoff is that the engineering group did not notify the quality group as soon as the modifications were suggested. Therefore, it is quite likely that no one has looked carefully at possible form, fit, or functional compatibility problems.

The product executive asked most of the right questions. We can only hope that he grabbed for the telephone and talked to the quality manager for an initial reaction. Then, he should have gotten together with responsible management, engineers, quality specialists, production, and purchasing people so they could all discuss the details. At the very least, it would seem that formal tests conducted with the quality people present are called for before committing the Spacefire to production. If the product executive doesn't take some positive action, the prognosis doesn't look good. **During design changes, it is easy to make things worse rather than better. Despite how minor the modifications may appear, the changes must be proven to work over a reasonable spectrum of product variables and stimulus variations.**

The Little Computer That Couldn't

The first solid-fuel ballistic missile was also the first one to take full advantage of the digital computer for missile guidance and control. Guidance, in particular, requires a rather sophisticated computer to take in information from the inertial guidance system and to calculate missile position, attitude, and velocity. The data generated is necessary for steering commands that keep the missile pointed in the right direction. There were several possible computer designs under study. The guidance contractor's preferred design, not surprisingly, was a modification of a computer in its inventory. The system engineering house hired by the Air Force to advise and critique the design had quite a different idea. It saw itself as a major supplier of missile hardware, so it formed its own computer design group and set out to create its version of the optimum ballistic missile computer.

The computer design proceeded apace. When the designers believed the design to be complete, it was described in copious detail bound up in a blue-covered binder. This was known ever after as "the Blue Book computer." The Blue Book computer used a rotating disc memory, as did the other competing computers. In such computers, the instructions and the data were all accessed in sequence from the rotating memory. This serial nature added a major dimension to the programming chore. The programmers of such machines had to know when to look for instructions and data, as well as where to look. The Blue Book computer was unique in that it was designed to read information continuously from the memory and process it whether the programmer ordered it at that time or not. As a result, it was able to correctly solve only a small set of very specific problems. Even so, it was necessary to lay out the problem very carefully to satisfy this odd and restrictive design. The workload had just been shifted dramatically from the computer hardware designer to the programmer. This did not bother the computer designers at all. They had eliminated gobs of transistors and electronic gates that would normally be used to control the memory access timing. Having cleverly done away with all that, the Blue Book computer was simpler and cheaper than competing computers, and it was clearly the computer of choice for the procurement people.

The system engineers had worked diligently to rigidly define the guidance and control problem while the design was progressing. From this data, they created the memory timing and the sample program to be used by Blue Book. Once the program was judged to be complete (nothing had been built yet, let alone tested), the design of the Blue Book computer was frozen. A feature of the design was that any subsequent change to the fixed timing was assured to be a major computer redesign.

Rational people began to wonder about the inflexibility of Blue Book. They were in the midst of a new solid-fuel missile design. Nothing like it had ever been built or flown. It was presumptuous to believe that enough was known to nail the control program down to the last bit at this stage in the development. The computer designers took the position that only the timing of the program instructions and the location of the data were unchangeable. Constants could be easily adjusted to accommodate variations in flight characteristics and profiles. Why fly a lot of decision-making hardware that won't be needed?

Why indeed? The system people had never before programmed a real-time, fixed-point serial computer. They knew nothing of the requirement to scale the data. Suffice it to say that it is always necessary to shift data right or left at several junctures to get the right answer. Shifting takes time. Blue Book did not allow for shifting time. The only problem that Blue Book was designed to solve was unsolvable by Blue Book. The programming supervisor working for the guidance contractor saw the flaw immediately at the first joint design review. Blue Book was quietly shelved. The guidance contractor's modified computer was accepted. A variation of that machine is still in the missile inventory today.

A lot of smart and subsequently successful people were involved in the concept and design of Blue Book. That the design got as far as it did is worrisome. In retrospect, inexperience and arrogance were mostly to blame. No one bothered to understand and solve pieces of either the guidance or the flight control problem as Blue Book would. After the first twenty minutes of such an exercise, the timing incompatibilities would have been self-evident.

Once again an elegant design came to an untimely end only days from committing it to production because the design managers didn't critically question the adequacy of the design. The same fundamental error is almost certainly happening somewhere else right now.

CHAPTER 5

Mistakes of Wrath

"I am willing to love all mankind—except an American."
- Samuel Johnson

MANAGERS HAVE A LOT OF THINGS they should do, probably an equal number of things they may want to do, but relatively few things they must do. **Regardless of what is done or why it is done, everything a manager does should be accomplished with strict impartiality.** A manager showing favoritism or antipathy is easily spotted. Even so, every day, odd decisions based on emotions rather than reason emerge from otherwise responsible management. These emotionally charged, hip-shot directions rarely seem to make good sense at the time, and in the light of subsequent events, often make no sense at all.

Several years ago I was involved in a six-week long running skirmish with a senior executive vice president, a division president, and a lesser light or two. My objective was to make right what appeared to be a serious wrong perpetrated against a technical writer. Reason finally prevailed, but at great cost. Here's the story.

The Famous Candy Machine Incident

During one of the last great aerospace layoffs, I found myself managing inertial instrument (gyroscope and accelerometer) design staff, hybrid microelectronics engineers, the odd inertial system project, and the Division Material and Process (M&P) laboratories. Managing these technically diverse people was more than enough to keep me busy. To make matters worse, the company was in the process of laying off hundreds of dedicated engineers because of funding reductions. Engineering managers needed no more problems, but a big problem created out of whole cloth was headed our way.

A technical writer working in the M&P laboratories felt a bit peckish on a fall afternoon. He sauntered over to the corner of the building to get a candy bar from a vending machine. As was common with our vending equipment, the machine swallowed his quarter (this happened some time ago) and disgorged no candy. He put in a second quarter with the same result. Understandably miffed, he sharply rapped the top of the evil machine with the heel of his hand.

Our maintenance people tended to be a little slipshod. One of their more unpleasant jobs was to clean behind the vending machines. To make that job easier, they pulled the machines well away from the wall, leaving them there so that a mop could easily get behind them. Unfortunately, the candy machines were designed to be placed flush against the wall. They had a six-inch foot protruding from the front, but no support in back. As the man rapped harder, the candy machine fell backward.

The vending area was located in a narrow hallway about as wide as the vending machines were high. As the machine gracefully slid against the wall, the base began to slide forward. Our hero was momentarily stunned. He froze while the machine pinned him against the opposite wall, sliding over one shoe and crunching his trapped foot.

He stood immobilized. No one came. He was on his own. He finally gritted his teeth, bent over, and after several painful tries was able to lift the machine base from his foot. He was hurt and embarrassed, but notified no one. He limped to his desk and went back to work, trying to concentrate on the specifications and ignore the pain, but it was not to be.

He finally called his wife and told her of his accident. The best she could offer was advice to go at once to the company dispensary for treatment. Her argument was a simple one. Since the problem was caused by a company machine, the company should do whatever was necessary to repair the damage to her husband's foot. Our tech writer hated to make waves in the existing environment where anyone with even a moderately negative profile was considered available for layoff, but he ruefully agreed to check in with the company nurse.

When he arrived at the dispensary, he found the nurse in a foul mood. The results were disastrous. With pursed lips she listened to his story, then asked him to remove his shoe. She found a badly scraped foot and bruised toes. She ordered the poor fellow into an examining room for what turned out to be an interrogation. The conversation, as best we could learn after the fact, went about as follows:

Angel-of-Mercy (AOM): "Tell me again, slowly, how you managed to do that to your foot."

Poor Tech Writer (PTW): "When the machine didn't produce any candy, I rapped on it, trying to get either my candy or my money back. The machine fell over backwards, then the base slid across the floor and onto my foot."

AOM: "You're telling me that the candy machine chased you?"

PTW: "No ma'am. There was a wall in the way. The machine couldn't fall straight back, so the top slid down the wall. I'm very sorry it fell, but it wasn't well supported."

AOM: "Our vending machines don't slide across floors. Did you kick that machine?"

PTW: "No Ma'am."

AOM: "I don't believe you! You deliberately kicked that machine! You are a vandal! You have a lot of gall to come to the company dispensary asking for my help after your malicious act."

PTW: "But, Ma'am!"

AOM: "Don't Ma'am me. I'm turning you into my boss, the head of labor relations! Don't expect any sympathy from him. I hope he fires you."

The AOM charged out. The PTW beat an immediate, but slow, retreat back to his desk.

One might be justified in believing that a nurse would try to ease a patient's suffering before concerning herself about her patient's transgressions. Not this lady. Also, for those who might think that labor relations people are those to whom an employee can turn in time of need, in this case, think again. Tom, the labor relations manager, wasn't sympathetic by nature. He had on several earlier occasions shown compassion worthy of Attila the Hun.

I never knew what set our AOM off. I still find it exceedingly difficult to believe that she gave one tinker's dam for the company or its property. There must have been more there than met the eye. No matter, the fat was now in the fire. Our PTW was in pain. The AOM was livid. Tom was about to have a new human target.

The AOM flounced into Tom's office with her story of the malicious damage to the candy machine. Unfortunately, our senior executive vice president, Harry, was there on another matter and heard her spin her irate tale. Harry must have had a bad hair day, too, because he gave an enthusiastic "Amen!" to the AOM's request and to Tom's subsequent pronouncement that the PTW should be fired forthwith.

Among the rarely read plant rules was one intended to discourage unauthorized or unfair employee terminations. It stated, in effect, that an employee's immediate supervisor must either initiate or agree with any termination action for cause. The PTW's immediate supervisor hadn't yet heard of the incident. His boss, the M&P laboratory manager had gone home for the day. I was on a business trip, as was my boss. Without talking to anyone in the engineering department, Tom gave orders to have the personnel records computer fire the PTW. So, of course, the computer fired him. So much for the rules.

The next day, while still in New York, I received a panic call from the M&P laboratory manager. He told me that Tom had personally fired one of M&P's tech writers without notifying anyone in the engineering department. Not knowing what had transpired, I tried to assure him that his man could not be fired, unless he and his supervisor concurred. He said that he sure hoped I was right because he was looking at a hand-carried termination notice from Personnel.

Figuring that this was just one more paper error, I called the personnel director, retelling the story that I had just heard. He assured me that he had heard nothing, suggesting that it was all an ugly rumor. When my boss and I discussed the matter over lunch, we agreed that Personnel had probably made another mistake. Given any luck, the problem would have disappeared by the time we were back.

No way. Once back, I found Tom had done his work well. In violation of company rules and reason, the PTW had been officially fired, and he didn't even know it yet. The next step was to talk to the PTW and get his version of the incident. I called him at home where he was nursing his foot. He repeated the story that he was blameless, with supporting detail about unstable candy machines. Next, I walked by the scene of the crime and found the evil candy machine back upright, but just barely. The machine was well away from the wall and leaning backward. I called our safety man. A quick look at the precarious candy machines was all he needed to order that they all be placed against the wall immediately before more fell over. Now that our candy machine instability was recognized by an independent observer as company-induced, I felt that the problem would go away rather quickly. Rational management would want to put things right once they found the company was at least partly at fault. The thing to do now was to spread the word. I called Tom. Never a pleasant task.

Me: "I hear you've fired one of our technical writers without the concurrence of engineering management. Why?"

Tom: "I don't need to explain my actions to you. Besides, I don't like the kind of outfit you are running. You have a violent company property destroyer in your midst, and you are defending him. I'm doing you a big favor by getting rid of a bad apple for you."

Me: All I know, or suspect, is that an order came from Personnel to M&P saying to fire a tech writer, and that both his supervisor and manager strongly disagree with that order. I also took the trouble to talk to the tech writer and to look at the vending machines. The machines were dangerously unstable. So dangerous that our safety man directed that they all be put back against the wall where they belong.

Tom: "All you need to know is that man has been fired for cause, whether you like it or not."

Me: "I don't like it! Did you talk to him before you got the computer to fire him?"

Tom: "I didn't need to. I got the go-ahead from Harry."

Me: "Did it ever occur to you that our tech writer might be the damaged party? Those machines were dangerous. This man is probably a victim of the incompetence of our maintenance people. He may have cause for a lawsuit because of that whether we fire him or not, but he is more likely to sue if you persist in this lunacy."

Tom: "You got a problem, you take it up with Harry."

Me: "If you don't fix this problem you and your people created, I will drop by the computer center and program your computer to fire you!" (I, too, can be subjected to moments of wrath. I could have been more diplomatic with Tom, but I doubt it would have helped much. Still, I should have tried.)

After this spirited exchange, it was clear that the engineering department had to enlist bigger guns. I called my boss and suggested that he call Harry before things got completely out of hand. Harry was unavailable. A persuasive senior scientist in my organization who heard of the problem became interested in seeing justice done. After an independent check, he also felt that the PTW was in the right. Better yet, this senior scientist played handball with Harry twice a week. Silly me, I still felt that reason would triumph if the facts as we knew them were known to Harry. So I asked my friend and colleague to discuss the matter with Harry after the handball game. He found to his surprise that the normally reasonable Harry was brooking no further discussion. He wanted our man not only fired, but also prosecuted. This was getting serious. The next move was unclear. We figured that under the circumstances we had best talk to the next higher person in our chain of command, the assistant general manager.

After a brief discussion, the assistant general manager understood the problem and promised to say a few kind words on our behalf to Harry, though he observed that this wasn't to be one of his more pressing issues. Shortly after our meeting, the assistant general manager mentioned the incident to his boss, the general manager while Harry was within earshot. Harry came over snarling, "If engineering management can spend time on this sort of thing, they are overstaffed and underworked." The general manager, Dick, immediately set up a meeting with all concerned with the intent of directing us to fire our writer forthwith. Dick's view was not a compassionate one. After perhaps thirty seconds of consideration, he became convinced that the PTW's dubious welfare wasn't worth any managerial dissension.

Even under the best of circumstances, meeting with Dick was risky. He was a man of quick temper and weak logic. We had already seen that there was something about this issue that had turned the normally mild Harry into a monster, and now we had Dick to contend with. We were running out of possible solutions. I might be able to get the computer to spit out some unauthorized paper firing Tom, and thus create sort of a bargaining chip, but as satisfying as that would be, it was likely to create still more trouble and probably not get the PTW unfired. It appeared that our PTW would be at the mercy of a man who was known to have simultaneously held as many as three conflicting positions.

DILBERT reprinted by permission of United Feature Syndicate, Inc.

Dick had advanced his career by continuously applying a single principle of cost control; that is, control headcount. In his view, all the time spent worrying about travel, communication, office materials, and the host of other costs is of little avail. If there aren't people around to travel, make phone calls, etc., costs tend to take care of themselves. This is all very well as long as cost reduction is the only goal. **The downside, of course, is that the real objective of business isn't to control costs but to create, market, and sell. This takes people. The ultimate cost cutter will go quietly out of business, happily achieving zero cost.**

We now found ourselves going against Dick's grain when we argued to retain yet one more head on a diminishing payroll, particularly when that head had already been sort of fired. During the meeting with Dick, we tried to defend the actions of our man as being perhaps unwise, but not malicious. We described probable lawsuits and resulting financial losses to the company if lawyers got hold of the incident, all the while passionately arguing for common justice. Dick initially dismissed all arguments out of hand. He knew he was in the right, after all, he agreed with Harry.

We reiterated the threat of legal action. We described the unfavorable publicity that could fall on the company. Dick began to waver a bit. We pressed on, observing that any bad publicity might well stick to various managers. For a time Dick was quiet. He appeared to be thinking about cutting his losses. When he spoke next, it was through clenched teeth. "It is against my better judgement, but since you feel so strongly, I will permit you to retain this vandal. He probably won't last long, but be advised that you have used up my good will." As we got up to leave before he changed his mind, he said, "Don't go yet. I have something more to say to you." We sat down. Dick faced us and pronounced "Remember, all of you, the only way to reduce cost is to reduce headcount!"

Meanwhile Tom had been having a few second thoughts. His boss, the personnel director, decided to get into the act. He quizzed Tom about this strange high visibility problem that was consuming so much executive time. When it became clear that not only had the PTW's supervisor refused to sign the termination order, but also three higher levels of engineering management strongly disagreed with Tom's position, the director suggested that in spite of Harry's verbal approval, Tom, for the sake of his career, might want to rethink his position. This left Tom feeling hung out, but he still had Harry on his side.

Meanwhile, Harry had been talking to Dick. They reinforced each other by blasting the conduct of engineers and engineering management. But now, having a better understanding of the situation, they were relieved to have this problem nearing a resolution. They realized that by reinstating the PTW as quietly as possible, the chances of the company being caught up in an expensive lawsuit would be lessened. At this point, they tacitly agreed to throw Tom to the wolves.

When Tom and Harry met, Harry said, "You must have misunderstood me. I intended for you to investigate the nurse's allegations and take whatever action you felt proper. Firing that man, as you did, violated at least one company rule. You must stand accountable." Tom left, stunned.

The next morning I had a call from Tom. It was a different Tom. He was polite. After a preamble of small talk, he asked if he were to have the PTW reinstated, could we put in a good word for him with the division management. I demurred, saying that after what had happened, few of our mutual bosses would be speaking to me for a while, if ever. Tom settled for a promise that I wouldn't cause anything strange to happen to his personnel file if he fixed things quietly.

A courier showed up with paper apparently intended to reinstate the PTW, but his name was misspelled. Even odder, the reinstatement paper was an authorization to hire him. This would not do. Had it been left unchallenged, our PTW would have lost his seniority and all that went with it.

It seemed that after executing Tom's illegitimate order, the computer had placed a permanent no-hire tag next to our PTW's name preventing his rehiring or reinstatement. This tag couldn't be removed without fiddling with the guts of the program. The staff that created the creaky old personnel records program had by now dispersed to the four winds. No one was available to make quick changes. Nearing desperation, Tom had tried a simple misspelling of the PTW's name. He had hoped that it might then be possible to fool the computer into reinstating this sort-of-fictitious person. The computer was ready for such shenanigans. It wouldn't allow reinstatement of someone whose name it didn't know, but it permitted the next best thing. It hired him.

The problem had now shifted from one of mollifying top management to one of mollifying the computer. Programmers diligently went to work trying various ploys to fake out the personnel records program so the "no-hire" tag could be purged. One could then begin with a more-or-less clean slate untainted by Tom's ire. It turned out not to be easy to do. It took time, the expenditure of several hours of computer time, and a lot of sweat but the PTW was finally reinstated with all except his U.S. savings bond withholding intact.

Neither the senior executive vice president nor the president ever forgot or forgave. Months later, after I had transferred to another division, I came back to discuss some open items with my successor. While at lunch in the dining room, aptly dubbed the "golden trough," Dick made a detour by my table to let me know how much he still resented the high-handed action I took to reinstate "that tech writing malcontent." By this time, as luck would have it, the poor fellow had been caught in one of the later lay-off cycles and was gone. His termination was legitimate, I hope.

Either noticeable damage was done to the operation of the company during the Famous Candy Machine Incident, or the involved managers were not having much impact in the daily running of the company. I prefer to think that all of us were useful people when we weren't at odds with each other. Perhaps we all learned something from the experience—perhaps.

The President, the Genius, and the Neanderthal

The semiconductor division of a large company was in deep trouble. Two short years before, the division had been the darling of the corporation, making profits hand over fist. This particular division had been a leader in the semiconductor chip and calculator business, having moved swiftly to take early advantage of the burgeoning market while competition was still limited. The division had even been profiting from selling electronic assemblies to the Japanese. For a time, the semiconductor division, together with a few other calculator chip manufacturers, basked in the worldwide shortage of electronic widgets. But the semiconductor industry was rushing headlong into more production capacity than the world needed at the time. This was the first of the cyclic business ups and downs that periodically distress semiconductor management and stockholders. Once this overcapacity was in place, sales and profit margins dropped everywhere. Incredible profits at the division had rapidly turned to jarring losses.

The corporate masters of our story had little real understanding of how the semiconductor business was evolving (not unlike many semiconductor executives today). Angered at what they perceived to be managerial incompetence, the corporate executives decided to combat the downward profit spiral by getting rid of most of the existing senior division managers. These losers would be replaced by new blood hired away from major semiconductor houses that had worked so diligently to create the industry-wide glut. The new people would be just the ticket to lead the division back to profitability. After years of managerial rotation and false starts, a complete opportunist was hired as the new division president. By this time, the semiconductor cycle was on the upswing. Games and personal computers were selling briskly. The fax machine market was just taking off. Semiconductor demand was again rapidly catching up with supply.

This newly hired president brought with him a set of cronies from Silicon Valley to help seize the reins and, if necessary, to take the fall. Rather surprisingly, there were few experienced managers in his entourage. The division had a critical need for a vice president of research and a director of manufacturing, but no one in the new group was even remotely qualified. Searches began for these valuable people. After considerable time and trouble, the president identified and hired a pair of individuals that seemed to satisfy his requirements. The first was a brilliant, but emotional, man who presently headed a successful semiconductor research group. The major drawing card used to lure him was the promise that he could manage a new state-of-the-art wafer fabrication line.

A manufacturing director was easier to find, although the president had quietly added a couple of his personal requirements. He wanted someone he could control. Someone who wasn't too bright, with just sufficient character to keep him from walking off with the elevator, and mean enough to put the fear of God into the president's perception of manufacturing people. The man he found was an individual with little discernable character, dim, loud, and filled with low cunning. The new man advertised to one and all that he believed in management by controlled aggression, but he later proved himself unable to control his aggressions.

The new aggressive manufacturing director sized up his management colleagues (or adversaries, as he thought of them), looking for those who would most easily succumb to intimidation. He put the new research VP at the top of his list. The VP had just begun to settle in. He had successfully, so far, grabbed hold of the reins of the new, and badly needed, wafer fabrication processes.

The president's weak character was beginning to show. Surprisingly, he proved to be easily intimidated by aggressive adversaries. It took the new manufacturing director some time to realize his potential power over the president, but when it finally dawned, he struck. He went out of his way to confront the president and other senior managers during a series of team-building sessions that the president had initiated to counteract growing management dissension. Despite the purpose of these sessions, executives began choosing sides, each trying to develop a power base that might support continued employment. The more perceptive of the managers were updating resumes.

The president, for a time, was able to deflect the snarls of the manufacturing director by laying blame on other executives for whatever ills were being bandied about. The research engineering and design engineering groups were the favorite targets. The research VP couldn't cope with the never-ending unfounded verbal barbs, so he opted out of team building. The president soon found that he had more important things to do than attend these sessions. When he came, he came late, observed the proceedings sans research VP, made occasional pithy pronouncements, and left early before the manufacturing director reached full crescendo. At this point, the manufacturing director decided that the time was right to make a go for his first power grab. He was sure that he had intimidated the research VP (and most of senior management) into inaction. His first move was a foray to usurp the management of the new wafer fabrication line.

There wasn't a subtle bone in the manufacturing director's body. He made an all out assault. He pointed out to the assembled engineering managers, minus the research VP, that no one had any concept of quality control or efficient production techniques, and that the division was fortunate that his manufacturing group could be persuaded to take over the new facility. Only his group could make the new line produce quality products, and then, only if the engineering designs were any good, which he doubted. When the president got wind of this attack, his first reaction was to sidestep it. He knew that the prime reason the research VP had taken the job he was so recently offered was his intense and abiding interest in developing new wafer fabrication processes in a cutting-edge facility. The research VP had publicly stated that he intended to make this fabrication line the showplace of industry, and he was making good progress toward that goal. However, the president's thoughts were governed by fear, and he was afraid to dismiss the manufacturing director's proposal. He did not want to be the butt of the cruel humor and wrath of the manufacturing director, so he equivocated. He called both the research VP and the manufacturing director together. First he assured himself that the manufacturing attempted power grab wasn't ugly rumor, but ugly fact. He then told the pair that his definite decision was that from now on, use of the new research fabrication line would be the joint responsibility of research and manufacturing. The details were to be worked out by those concerned. The manufacturing director beamed. He had no doubt that he would run over the research VP at will.

The very next day, the research VP found a manufacturing supervisor giving orders to a pair of process engineers. When the VP asked for an explanation, the supervisor rather sheepishly admitted that his boss had ordered him to take over a part of the line. He went on to say that his director had announced to lower-level managers that the president had decided the manufacturing group would be in charge. The VP couldn't believe his ears. He dashed over to see the president, who wasn't in, at least not for him. Failing to find anyone who could explain what was happening, the VP went away to lick his wounds. He asked himself if the manufacturing director was really pulling the rug out from under the research group, or was this simply an honest misunderstanding?

When the president deigned to see his VP, he equivocated once again. The president said, "I'm sure that something was lost in the translation. What I said was that there should be close cooperation between the research and manufacturing groups. Perhaps manufacturing supervision became a little eager and overstepped its authority. Rest assured you are in charge of the fabrication line. The manufacturing group is there to help." By now, the VP had his president calibrated. He knew the president often spoke with a forked tongue, but armed with words he wanted to hear, the VP decided to try to straighten out what might be the manufacturing director's misconception. He felt it was essential to the well-being of the division and to his own well-being to keep the manufacturing group out of the research group's business.

Our crafty director was just leaving for the day when the VP caught up with him and related the latest pronouncement of the president. The director was completely unimpressed. He irately dismissed the VP out of hand, telling him, "The president was handing you a line. He wants me to take over the new wafer line and instill some discipline. If I have any more trouble from you about who is running that line, I will have you fired." Having said his piece, he turned on his heel and left.

The poor VP was in shock. He made a final half-hearted attempt to see the president, hoping against hope that perhaps the whole thing was the result of massive confusion. The president made himself unavailable. Ultimately frustrated, the vice president left a note pinned to the president's door. It said, "I won't take this kind of treatment. I quit."

And so he did. The genius packed his belongings that night and never returned. His prior company was very glad to get him back. As for the Neanderthal manufacturing director, he had little idea of what it took to run a wafer line. Under his direction, things went from good to very bad. Finally, the president was forced to ask an experienced corporate process team to fix the mess. The president knew that the VP's abrupt departure and the resulting need to ask for corporate help reflected unfavorably on his own management ability, which was something he knew he must decisively correct. It was now essential that the Neanderthal director be removed and replaced as quickly as possible. If the director remained unscathed, not only would it appear to corporate headquarters that the wrong man had won, but the divisiveness within his division would likely get worse as the manufacturing director selected and attacked his next victim.

The president began a whispering campaign to rid himself of this now well-identified millstone. He encouraged his other executives to alternately ignore and insult the hated director. When none of this had the desired effect, the president plotted to get rid of his Neanderthal hire by remote control, hoping that only a little mud would end up clinging to his own boots. He sent the Neanderthal to a pair of important corporate briefings with obsolete information, allowing him to infuriate the big boss not once, but twice. Shortly after those exchanges, corporate headquarters ordered the firing of the manufacturing director. The president's resignation followed shortly thereafter.

The prime responsibility of this debacle lay with the president. The manufacturing director was what he was. His selection was a terrible mistake. Once he had been hired, **the president compounded the problem by failing to give him and others clear direction,** allowing ire and chicanery to take over. The Neanderthal felt that he had tacit authority to make his run at the new line. **The president's total failure to take strong and immediate corrective action converted a nasty situation into a disaster.**

CHAPTER 6

Paper Costs

*"I am not an editor and shall always try to do right
and be good, so that God shall not make me one."*
- Mark Twain

Writing too much is generally much worse than writing too little.

ORDERLY ORGANIZATIONS can sustain measurable damage from attempts to manage principally by the written word, relying on verbose directives to provide management information. A few written directives, policies, or procedures answering common questions or stating a few important rules for all to see can be useful. However, to allow these pieces of paper to grow into a blizzard of words and then expect them to manage for us is quite wrong. The penalties paid for the overuse of these management aids aren't always the obvious. The costs of the blank paper, the ink, and the salaries of the policy writing group(s) are trivial when compared to the damage done through errors and misunderstandings.

Despite the questionable results stemming from management by the book, a near-universal feeling of worth, almost a reverence, for the written word persists which is at best uncertain, and at worst unjustified. **Words on paper must be cogent, read, and fully understood before becoming bases for actions.** Minimizing the volume of written procedures and the like is an essential management job. The trick is to come close to the optimum point.

People make errors resulting from acting on unclear, missing, conflicting, or wrong words they have read. Commonly, there is redundancy (sometimes tridundancy) inevitably leading to confusion and conflict among the redundant words. **Managers should scrupulously avoid duplicating information in written procedural material.**

The Charter Maker

Not long ago, a new CEO of a Fortune 500 company decided that to focus the activities and decisions of management, the company needed a formal charter. He established an executive committee to create just the right words. After a week or so of haggling, the chairman of the committee, amid fanfare, published a one-half page charter for all to see. It extolled company goals and was particularly explicit about enhancing profits. Once published, the company employees read more into the profit emphasis than had been intended. Worse, some busybody determined that portions of the new charter more or less disagreed with three of twenty-five existing policies residing in the company policy manual. Even though policy manuals were everywhere, they were little read, had been unchanged for years, and unfortunately, hadn't been considered by the executive committee that created the charter. Where the company policies emphasized quality of output and fair treatment of employees, the new charter clearly stated that returns on investment and sales were the two most important company goals. Since the policy manual was expected to reiterate and expand the charter notions, selective revision was considered necessary.

Revising the policy manual was a rather touchy issue. After publishing the new charter, the company grapevine was busy repeating rumors that product quality and employee welfare would be soon on the block in order to enhance profits. The new words in the policy manual must agree with the charter, while at the same time, allay employee fears that the charter was a harbinger of cost cutting and downsizing.

It took several months to carefully review and revise the offending policies. When the administration manager noticed that some of these revised and approved policies were now in conflict with other polices, he received permission to hire a policy expert to sort it all out. The whole process took about a year and consumed many hours in corrections, reviews, and re-reviews before the new policy manual was published.

Company employees were now reading the policy manual, most of them for the first time. They read more into the revised policies than had been intended. This worried them even more than the words in the charter. Furthermore, several busybodies determined that portions of the new policy manual conflicted with about one hundred of the more than four-hundred procedures of the four-volume company procedures manual. Even though these procedures manuas were everywhere, they were little read, and unfortunately, hadn't been considered by management, the policy expert, or the writers hammering out the policies. Since the pro-cedures manual was expected to reiterate and expand the policy notions, a major revision of the manual was considered necessary. The policy expert was soon on the trail of various obscure and often conflicting divisional policies and procedures, guides, and manuals, all needing work to bring them into line with the higher tier documents and with each other.

During this process, a new CEO was hired who believed that revising the charter statement would enhance the company management philosophy. He established an executive committee to create just the right new words...here we go again.

When management relies on paper for decision making, it takes on a life of its own, spawning ever more pages despite valiant efforts by more rational managers to curtail them. The unaccounted costs incurred by managers can be extensive. They must discuss, review, and yes, even write things like policies, charters, and mission statements. **The time is better spent giving people clear direction and the tools they need to work.**

Pity the poor new hire! In a busy environment, few can be bothered with befriending and training a new individual. All of the effort expended to finally get the right person to accept employment may go for naught in the first two weeks unless management steps in and takes a firm hand. The new employee needs friendship and information about the new job. Unfortunately, the people who know their way around well enough to offer capable guidance are usually key folks in constant demand, so more often than not, this valuable human asset is left alone and given a set of manuals to read.

Despite the time taken to read manuals, the most useful information acquired by the new hire comes directly from management or peers as the new employee catches them on the fly. This benign neglect is to blame for the unrecognized loss of many potentially productive hours in otherwise well-managed organizations, not to mention the loss of the good people who simply go elsewhere because they feel unused and unwanted. The typical human resources/personnel department doesn't help a great deal either. My friends in various senior management positions concur with surprising unanimity that obligatory human resources indoctrinations are generally based on company manuals and training aids that are too often outdated and irrelevant.

Managers must take the time to hold face-to-face informational discussions with all new employees. Just as first impressions are found to be the most lasting in individual relationships, first impressions of a company, its management, and its staff are the strongest for the new employee. Paper does not substitute for human contact.

With the widespread belief that more volume and detail equal more substance, comes a question commonly asked when investigating the causes of any troublesome occurrence. It is, "Was the proper action covered in sufficient detail by written procedures?" This query should be changed to ask, "Were insufficient training, poor motivation, bad supervision, lack of proper tools, or other reasons the root cause or contributing factor?" Puttying up procedures without changing something real won't help. During a postmortem, procedures are examined in detail and are usually found wanting. The offending sections are then examined and rewritten to correct this most recent failing. Chances are good that new errors will be introduced when writing, and the stage will be set the next investigation.

Another common belief is that more procedural detail will always help to further constrain unwanted employees actions. Added detail will probably do more harm than good, but writing a few important things down can help to clear one's thoughts. **Written policies and procedures are all substitutes for thinking, training, or personal contact. The thicker the policy manual, the weaker the company management is likely to be.**

For reasons as yet undetermined, organizations with strong dependencies on policies and procedures are also likely to rely heavily on motivational exercises to bond the employee to the company and to improve employee morale, productivity, or something else. The combination of too little thought, too many policies, and too much motivation can produce some surprisingly unpleasant results.

The Disappearing Engineers—A Modern Fairy Tale

Once upon a time, a moderately sized privately held company involved in designing and producing technological wares was awarded a number of new development and production contracts. This company's products were distinguished from its competitors' by highly innovative designs. These designs were the output of a top-notch and highly motivated group of about fifty engineers. In addition to their creativity, these engineers felt a sincere responsibility for their designs long after the drawings and specifications were released. To make sure that the products behaved as designed, the engineers made a point of supporting the factory people whenever it appeared that engineering skills were needed. To the chagrin of the administration, most engineers cared less for proper time charging than they did for attacking and solving problems as they arose, often requiring the cooperative effort of everyone in the group. The administrators were continually dismayed by the poor financial discipline of this engineering group.

With the award of several lucrative contracts, the CEO, spurred on by his staff, decided he needed to exercise better control over his soon-to-grow

engineering group. He was convinced that the written policies and procedures he and his staff were relying on to run the company were too few
and too short, and, therefore, inadequate. He honestly felt that procedures
actually controlled something, so he decided to use some of the new contract money to hire more people to write more procedures. This would
surely provide for better management while requiring fewer managers.

To further hone his management skills, the CEO had recently attended a
very satisfying seminar series. He had learned a great deal about motivational programs, and how the rank and file of the company could be persuaded to work harder for pens and plaques instead of money.

The CEO set about hiring an individual with extensive experience in policy
writing and motivational techniques to direct this new and vital activity.
As it happened, a wizard with a perfect background had just become
available. He was between jobs and came highly recommended as a
specialist in control and motivation by the head of the group presenting
the motivational seminars. The CEO was so impressed by the wizard's
credentials that he hired him on the spot, giving him the exalted title
of Motivational Expert.

The CEO advised the wizard that his first and most important assignment
would be to instill a respect for authority in the engineering group. They
were far too freewheeling. They must be brought to heel, and soon. This
fit well with the wizard's views. He had never liked engineers very much.
Being a wizard, he felt he was far better. Engineers hadn't treated him
with the respect he felt he deserved. He felt about engineers much as the
British felt about the GIs in World War II—they were "over paid, over-
sexed, and over here." So, armed with his new staff, the wizard set out
to improve the productivity of the engineering group, at the same time
instilling in them a little fear.

The wizard sprung from a family of sorcerers. His Transylvanian forefathers
had been in the magic and motivational business for eons. For now, he had
possession of the family Manual, which contained a plethora of magical
motivational sayings, acronyms, and incantations. Advice taken from its
gilded pages had been used by King George III to develop the policy of
governing his American colonies. The Manual's words had inspired

Napoleon's army at Moscow while slogging through the snow. The French general's staff had consulted the Manual when deciding the defensive policies of France prior to World War II. Results could have been better, but the wizard laid all the blame on the Europeans, particularly the French.

As time passed, the fortunes of the wizard's family had declined, forcing the wizard to immigrate to the United States where he had formed a temporarily successful consulting group. For a time after World War II, the wizard had provided charters, incantations, policies, and management seminars for American steel-producing giants.

Once hard at work for our CEO, the wizard and the Manual conspired to bring to the American industrial world a long-dormant motivational program. The basis for this beautiful work was the human relations philosophy of no less than Marie Antoinette. The name of this royally inspired wisdom was PRIDE (Personal Responsibility In Daily Effort). The details of a brilliantly planned PRIDE program had lain unused between the covers of the magic Manual for much too long. Now the PRIDE program and all of its motivational power could be unleashed on the world.

The many benefits of the PRIDE program panacea were touted to the receptive owner and his staff in a fine multimedia briefing using 150 interactive multicolored screens. The CEO, impressed by the sheer beauty and magnitude of the presentation, instantly believed in the potential value of PRIDE, and ordered it instituted immediately. Flushed with the success of selling PRIDE, the wizard went on to outline his plan to create some 200 new policies and procedures that he felt would be a good start for introducing discipline to the rabble. He received a standing ovation from the senior management.

It took time for PRIDE-related banners, award plaques, and other sundries to be ordered, produced, and delivered. For a time, the only noticeable effect that the work of the wizard, the Manual, and the new policy and procedures group had on company performance was to divert the attention of working management. The policy writers scurried about with armloads of questionnaires for all engineers to complete at once. Without this important information in hand, the policy and procedures writers weren't even able to begin writing. At first, the engineers were cooperative. The word had been passed that these odd activities had the blessing of the front office. Then, the first of the policies and procedures showed up. The policy title was *Proper Time Expenditure and Accounting for Engineers.* The procedure title was *Creating and Recording Engineering Time Charges, Definitions of, Methods for, Approvals Required, and Penalties for Non/Late/Incorrect Recording.*

Buried in the new procedure were a series of requirements anathema to engineers. Time clocks were to be installed to monitor the engineers' comings and goings. In addition to punching time clocks morning and evening, all engineers would need a pass from a manager to leave the plant at lunch. Another provision required each engineer to enter on each time card all hours worked to the nearest tenth of an hour. Authorization sheets containing long series of multidigit charge numbers were to be given out each week. All time entered was required to be associated with at least one of these numbers, and in an easy-to-read color code—black for paid straight time, red for overtime paid at the one and one-half straight time rate, blue for double time, and green for time worked for no pay. Charge account numbers were to be entered by the engineers in the same color as the associated time entries. The hours worked in support of each charge number were to be summarized by each engineer at the end of each day, again to the nearest tenth of an hour. At first, the engineers couldn't comply because they hadn't enough red, blue, and green pencils to mark the cards. This created havoc with the time card auditors. The wizard immediately ordered specially constructed ballpoint pen systems with the word PRIDE engraved on them for each engineer. These were truly complex and imaginative instruments. Each one contained three individual pens that could be uncovered at will with the flick of a switch. Unfortunately, the pens wrote only in black, red, and blue. The wizard couldn't find any green. The engineers would just have to figure out on their own where to get green.

In the ensuing weeks, engineering time cards were audited on a random basis to insure that all charge numbers were filled in and all time recorded was current to the day. Any engineer caught with a non-compliant time card would suffer a one-month delay in salary review. Surprisingly, most of the engineers tried to comply, believing that if they went along for a while, rational people would see the folly and the whole thing would fade away. The system was costing a pretty penny, and no good seemed to be forthcoming. The engineers weren't doing anything different than before, except working less on technical assignments while expending a great deal of effort filling out time cards. People who had often worked long hours without compensation, now didn't. For one thing, they had no green pens to record the time. One manager and two engineers left for less troublesome pastures.

The PRIDE material finally arrived. It had taken longer than the wizard had promised. The motivational material was late and flawed. One gross of plaques arrived labeled PRIZE, another PRICE, and yet another BRIBE. Finally, the wizard was able to initiate the PRIDE program with fanfare and huzzahs. A huge PRIDE banner was hung from the company head-quarters building. PRIDE award meetings abounded. PRIDE posters con-taining pithy sayings like, "When the going gets tuff, the tuph get going" graced the walls. (Spelling was never one of the wizard's strengths.) PRIDE plaques were handed out by the dozen to any employee found doing the least dollop of good work. By the fourth week of the program, it was the unusual secretary that didn't have at least two PRIDE plaques hanging above her desk. PRIDE was everywhere.

With the joint successes of PRIDE and the *Proper Time Expenditure and Accounting for Engineers* policy, the wizard turned to the more difficult task of improving engineering productivity. This effort would certainly require hundreds more policies and procedures. A crash program resulted in the disgorging of the first procedure in just days. The title was *Productivity and Work Ethics, Minimum Standards for, Measurement of, and Disposition of Personnel Failing to Meet Standards*. The wizard and the Manual, feeling all warm about PRIDE, decided that another acronym would do wonders. So before this latest procedure hit the engineers' desks, AIM (Analyze, Improve, Measure) was created. AIM was to be the title of the new productivity measurement system. Logically, AIM should have been MAI (Measure, Analyze, Improve), but AIM sounded a lot jazzier than MAI.

AIM was a program conceived with malice, and it involved using writers and motivators to measure the productivity of engineers. The writers and motivators were understandably delighted. They had been presented with a golden opportunity to observe and criticize. If they could show that the engineers were not working as hard as they might, salary money might flow from the engineering coffers into theirs. The engineers decided to keep their collective sense of humor while fending off the attack. When the monitors arrived with stopwatches and clipboards to measure engineering productivity, the engineers were ready for them. The engineers had created an elaborate early warning system to announce the impending arrival of the productivity measurers.

To insure these assessments would be as favorable to the engineers as possible, an AIM actors' guild was formed within the engineering group. Directors were assigned to coach the engineers on how to look busy and highly productive. By listening to a pair of monitors talking shop, an engineer found that a surefire method of being rated highly productive was to be holding a technical conversation on the telephone when the monitors showed up. When alerted, two-thirds of the staff reached for the telephone. It all worked swimmingly. It might not have worked quite so well if the monitors had noted that there were only seven separate telephone lines shared by some fifty people. For the month following the introduction of this new procedure, the lion's share of engineering effort was expended in confounding the evaluators. One manager and five engineers decided to pack it in.

The measurement games got old. The engineers really wanted to get things done, but as soon as they were deep into a complex problem, either the monitors or motivators would show up. Morale was very low. A SHAME (Somebody Has Alienated Most Engineers) program was introduced to counter the PRIDE program, which now pervaded the company and even its restrooms. The soap dispensers contained labels saying "Push lever - Receive soap - Imbue hands and face - Dry - Enjoy effective cleaning." In the engineering department, posters appeared from nowhere reading, "Ready, AIM, Fire."

In the midst of this increasing chaos, another procedure was published. Its title was *Staff Improvement, Program for:*. The wizard and his procedures people, who were becoming ever more assertive, had convinced executive managers that the recent sharp drop-off in useful engineering output was due to incompetent engineers being retained by silly engineering managers. (The wizard made this assertion despite the consistently high engineering productivity that was being measured through the AIM program). One company director suggested that part of the problem might be the lack of competent replacements for those who had inexplicably quit. The wizard dismissed this thought out of hand. The solution was obvious, hence the latest procedure.

The *Staff Improvement Program Procedure* called for a quota of engineers to be terminated every three months for cause. This would soon set things right. The wizard knew in his bones that in any engineering organization there are always people who deserve to be fired. He told the CEO, "The only reason those people are still around is that engineering management is chicken. What's more, there will be a double benefit. Besides getting rid of the deadwood, the engineers who survive will be scared silly and will go back to work with a vengeance." Another acronym was needed. The wizard checked with the Manual. The Manual checked with the netherworld, and SIP for Staff Improvement Program was born.

The wizard held several unsatisfactory meetings with engineering management trying to promote the benefits of SIP. The managers were having none of it. As engineering management became surly, and then unruly, the wizard became ever more certain of the correctness of his actions. He was clearly dealing with malcontents. He exhorted his staff to write faster.

By now, the engineers had decided that things were definitely not going their way. They cast about, both individually and collectively, for other employment. As it happened, the first manager to leave had been funded by astute venture capitalists and now had her own engineering company. Even though it was small and new, she had been awarded two development subcontracts. She needed a number of good engineers. During a lunchtime gathering with several of her old management friends, she offered to hire any or all of the people from the now dwindling group who would care to join her. The managers took the word back to the engineers. After a brief discussion and vote, the engineering group elected to leave en masse and join the new company. As one, they gave notice.

The CEO had been uneasy for some time. Customer complaints about slipshod work and slipping production schedules had reached a crescendo.

When the chief engineer notified the CEO of the group's decision to quit, it came as yet one more piece of bad news. It seemed to the CEO that good engineering might be needed now more than ever. He called for his wizard to put things right. The wizard advised him not to worry, dismissing the loss of the engineers as a matter of little importance, and possibly as a good thing. Payroll costs would be reduced significantly. He explained that the exodus of the engineers was the human equivalent of rats running down the hawser on their way to shore. The CEO was leery, but the wizard muttered a minor soporific incantation and everyone felt better. When the soon-to-be ex-chief engineer asked about an orderly transition, the CEO prompted by the wizard, directed that the engineers could leave at any time. The wizard promised that his motivators and writers could easily finish the unfinished research tasks. After all, they would no longer be tied up measuring the productivity of the engineers. Besides, he had recently hired 15 more specialists. In order to expedite all of this, the wizard started 25 more procedures.

The factory badly needed engineering help. The factory manager pleaded for assistance. The wizard, who was now the *de facto* chief engineer, swung into action. In short order, a writer and two motivators showed up in the factory. They called a meeting with factory managers and told them how well they were treated. They also strongly suggested that factory managers were remiss in not solving their own problems. The writer even offered to write a procedure summarizing problem-solving techniques. So they tried, but procedures and motivation weren't what the factory needed. As more trouble occurred, the factory managers tried work-arounds that sometimes helped, but as more and more problems surfaced, workarounds just weren't enough. The factory began to shut down, station by station.

It was now dawning on the CEO that his problems were very serious. The dawn came too late. Vital deliveries were missed. Contracts were canceled. Lawsuits were filed. Since the factory was now virtually stopped, droves of production employees were laid off. All of the procedure writers were pressed into service, but to no avail. Since they couldn't fix or run anything, they wrote several procedures. One established rules for assigning executive parking places. Another entitled *Controlled Factory Shut Down, Directions for: Signatures Required* was sent out for coordination.

In desperation, the CEO placed a group of pricey consultants under contract with explicit instructions to bring order out of chaos. They assessed the cause of the debacle, and wrote an excellent report assigning blame to various internal organizations. Principally named were the now non-existent engineers. The report concluded with the recommendation that experienced engineers, familiar with both products and production techniques, be hired at once. A second and final report was nearly complete when the company went bankrupt. Had the report been completed, it would have been a great help in identifying several competitive issues, while outlining marketing strategies for the upcoming five-year planning cycle.

The owner began to understand the value of trained and dedicated people who would work the right problems at the right time. He pleaded with the wizard to put things back the way they were before he came. The wizard flew into a rage. He could see all his good work going down with the company. Hundreds of policies and procedures would die stillborn. The waste! The shame!

The wizard consulted with the Manual. The wizard and the Manual figured it was once again time to move on. They had seen it all before. They told themselves they had done everything right. The wizard had been thwarted at every turn. People were just no good. Even the surefire PRIDE and AIM programs had failed. (SIP was always considered to be a bit iffy). The wizard considered casting a major spell on all engineers but decided against it. He had once beautifully chanted a complex incantation, which should have made him a senior vice president of General Motors. His accent must have gotten in the way. After that traumatic experience he attempted only minor spells, but he was still well-prepared for the present situation. He had taken the precaution of getting his resume out early, even before the problems became acute. As a result, the wizard and the Manual easily found an excellent joint executive position at a major software company on the strength of their highly successful efforts to bring discipline to an otherwise chaotic engineering group. They wrote outstanding resumes.

The CEO was not so fortunate. His company was no more. It had been his life. He had nowhere to go. The night the company shut down was dreary and bitter cold. Sleet, swirled about by the chill wind, drove into the corners of the empty black parking lot and drifted against the now useless light poles. Hundreds of pages of loose and useless procedures swept across the bare lot, caught by the chain-link fence. The remnants of the PRIDE banner, shredded by the freezing winds, flapped from the black headquarters building. The shivering little man tucked his thin cloth coat about him calling and searching the parking lot for his lost engineers. The howling wind drowned out his voice and whipped the coat about his legs. Half out of his mind, he thought he could hear an engineer, or perhaps two, striding across the parking lot to his rescue. He could see nothing in the inky blackness so he lit a match, then another, and then another.

They found him in the morning, frozen, with only his coat and a torn piece of the PRIDE banner gathered about him. His face was covered with wet, sticky policy statements and procedures. Beneath his scorched fingers were piles of burned matchsticks.

Much of this story truly happened, fairy tale, or no. There was never a wizard, though there were several people who auditioned for the part. There was a PRIDE, an AIM, and a SIP. There was a Manual—not just one, but shelves of manuals and huge policy and procedure tomes. Woe to the manager who was ignorant of the wisdom dripping from its hallowed pages! Unfortunately, the real Manual met with about the same degree of success as the one in the fairy tale.

The planning and writing of charters, policies, and procedures is an arcane art and should only be done by skilled professional people. It takes skill to produce policies and procedures that can be read and acted upon without being counterproductive. Most organizations can get by nicely without any charter statements and only a few written policies. A limited number of properly written procedures can be useful. Webster's dictionary defines a policy as "a governing principle", and a procedure as "a particular course of action." Webster also astutely includes "artfulness" and "cunning" as descriptors of a policy. It seems as if Noah had a premonition of the content of some of our modern company policies.

Valuable procedures are those that clearly describe useful actions. Virtually all procedures might be easily renamed *Instructions* and procedure manuals renamed *Instruction Handbooks*. Activities like often-run chemical analyses, operation of computer programs, repair of all kinds of vehicles and equipment, company drawing and communications standards, data entry of all sorts, most product assembly and test procedures, and document classification and retention can all benefit by having clearly written detailed instructions. Orientation and training classes can materially benefit from the use of well-written and current instructions dealing with the subjects at hand.

Virtually all procedures suffer from a lack of quantitative writing. It is so much easier to insert words like "proper," "appropriate," or "useful," than it is to research and include the real conditions like "three feet," five RPM," or less than $3000.00. **Vague words have no place in procedure writing and should be totally excluded. When the specifics aren't known, there isn't enough to include it in any manual.** A few "To Be Determined's" may be fine for a brief period while things are being sorted out. Even then, a range of values ought to be entered to help the reader until the real conditions can be determined.

Rules for Creating Charters, Policies, Procedures, and Other Dangerous Things

Rule 1. Don't bother spending time creating charters by consensus because it's usually wasted time.

Rule 2. All policies should be independent from one another.

Rule 3. No organization ever needs more than ten independent statements of policy (e.g., the Ten Commandments).

Rule 4. No single written policy should be more than one page long.

Rule 5. Policies and procedures are quite different one from another. They should never contain the same information.
(Rules 2 and 5 are both cases of the larger truth: **Information and data should only be written once in any formal set of documents.**)

Rule 6. Procedures and instructions should never be vague. They must be specific to be useful.

Whoever violates these rules is responsible for having authorized or created too much paper, or for having said the same thing in two or more places, and for a myriad of reasons, failed to be clear. Even if the gods are favorable and everything is set down correctly the first time, chances are the updates or alterations will be missed or misread. These writings may now be a source of confusion to the careful reader, and the costs will be greater than just the paper they are written on.

CHAPTER 7

When All Else Fails, Tell the Truth

"It is hard to believe that a man is telling the truth when you know that you would lie if you were in his place."
- H. L. Mencken

MODERN MANAGEMENT CONSULTANTS, marketing theorists, and the occasional psychologist have made millions of dollars playing to our frailties. While most of their work is well-intentioned and much of it can be made useful, it tends to create and follow ever-changing fads. **Most motivational programs are intended to make us behave in ways beneficial to someone other than ourselves.** Ads, seminars, and the like try to convince us to buy something we may not need, to elect someone who is often less than the best, or to support uncertain causes. Advertising commonly relies on the substitution of tricks and canned ploys for facts and honest reasoning. As a result, we have become justifiably cynical and suspicious of any idea presented to us. Managers who rely on clever, but less than honest, techniques to motivate people are rather quickly spotted. With their credibility called into question, such managers are very likely to have more than their share of people problems.

I reported briefly to a general manager whose reputation was so sordid that a major customer we had been courting refused to do business with us once our division was transferred into his operation. When our potential customer learned of the identity of the new boss, he said through his teeth, "We have found that man's word to be utterly worthless. Any contract he controls is no contract at all. We won't do business with you as long as you are reporting to him." This was a bitterly disappointing turn of events to those of us who had worked very hard to capture this new business. C'est la guerre. There was nothing we could do.

People who are less than honest, but none too adept (some might say intellectually challenged) at it, usually don't represent a serious threat. Fortunately, they are caught early by those who are less challenged. But smart and dishonest managers can be extremely dangerous. These individuals can further their aims in subtle (and not so subtle) ways that are hard to foresee and even harder to combat. The following is a case in point.

Moving Day

A senior executive of a think tank that recruited engineering talent ordered the conversion of a bull pen area inside the company's office. Instead of the one hundred closely packed desks it could hold, it now sported spacious cubicles for forty engineers. The clerestory windows provided filtered light. The walnut-paneled walls, matching oiled walnut furniture, leather-covered chairs, and indirect lighting were unmatched outside of executive suites of the time. As particularly talented applicants visited the facility, they were greeted and then treated to a tasty lunch at the local gourmet restaurant. Afterwards, they were shown this fabulous area. As they walked through, they would see their name plate on one of the cubicles. When asked, the guide (an attractive lady if the applicant was male, a handsome man if the applicant was female) would observe that if the applicant accepted the company's offer, that cubicle would be reserved for the applicant. More than one outstanding Ph.D. succumbed to the lure.

When the newly hired arrived, they were ensconced in these sumptuous quarters. Until the area filled, the scene replayed itself forty times. As soon as all of the desks were occupied, a manager came by to tell the group that it would be necessary to move to more mundane quarters in a bull pen area while some necessary safety modifications were being made.

Days later, curious about when they could move back in to the best of all possible office areas, a pair of engineers stopped by to see how construction was coming. Other than being empty, the area looked no different than when they had moved out, except for a strange nameplate on one of the cubicles. As they were leaving a delightful young lady entered with an applicant in tow saying, "When you come to work for us this will be your cubicle." The inquisitive engineers both gave written notice terminating their relationship with the company.

About half of the engineers stayed with the company for at least a year knowing that they had been successfully conned, so the ploy worked. There were three or four waves of applicants trapped by the office lure during this period, but the company paid a penalty over time. The executive responsible for the ploy carried a reputation for dishonesty with him ever after. Like elephants, engineers rarely forget.

Crafty managers can often fool the big boss for extended periods, but they have a much harder time fooling their peers and those who work for them. **Crafty managers may look better from the top down than they do from the bottom up, but they are headed for trouble.** Never discount the power of people acting in concert. Employees can do more damage to a manager's effectiveness and reputation than most managers realize. When confronted with blatant management dishonesty, particularly when their livelihoods are affected, workers can band together, acting like a pride of lions.

If we could always trust the actions and words of others, management problems would be simplified a great deal. Unfortunately, we cannot take words at face value. There are a few postulates we can call on to make life a bit easier, though.

Most people shade the truth to their advantage on occasion, but few go in for the big lie.

It is the rare individual who reports that things he or she is responsible

for are worse than they really are (except when he or she has just taken over). Therefore, the wise manager will look for things to be moderately worse than most people say they are.

In the case of a manager in a new position, one can't be sure. A slightly dishonest new manager may, after a jaundiced evaluation of the state of the organization, tell the boss or the board of directors, "Things were so poorly run by the previous manager that I may not have arrived in time to save things. All of my expertise must now be called upon to save the company from the prior incompetence." I know of a CEO who has gotten away with this rather spurious and self-serving argument three different times.

An example of the problems less-than-honest managers can create for their companies is the subject of the next story. This company's managers paid little attention to facts. Instead, they began believing their own customer briefings. They tried to pull the wool over the eyes of some key employees and their customer at the same time.

Star Bright

This tale is about an irascible naval captain, a malfunctioning star tracker, and a field service technician left twisting in the wind. Good field service technicians are the salt of the earth and among the most maltreated. Those with even a few years of experience can, at the drop of a hat, regale compatriots with tales of being sent by the home office into a den of jackals with no more than a loincloth, having been told they would only face a cote of lambs. Out of sight, out of mind.

In the early 1960s, a company called Trackers Unlimited was under contract to the U.S. Navy to provide a precision star tracker for navigation on board ships. The contract was awarded to Trackers Unlimited because they promised better performance and faster delivery than their competition. They also demonstrated pieces of an experimental, almost working, tracker to the Navy brass to justify the preeminent position touted in their briefings.

Once the contract was let, prototype tracker fabrication and assembly began in earnest. As work progressed, it became evident to the engineering staff of Trackers Unlimited that there were real problems with the basic optics design. A quick series of conferences were called to figure out what to do. The engineering director, embarrassed and coerced by general management, decided to gamble by replacing the proposed and partially demonstrated tracker hardware with a potentially superior and technically interesting untried design. So the engineers embarked on a crash change to the tracker drive and optics.

Trackers Unlimited didn't want the word to get around that they weren't nearly as far ahead of their competition as they had let on. The management decided that anyone not directly involved with the design and fabrication of the new tracker should be kept in the dark regarding the massive redesign and resulting technical progress (or lack of it). Those out of the know, of course, included the field service technicians and the Navy. Trackers Unlimited management figured that if the field service technicians knew the truth, it was likely the Navy would soon learn the ugly facts as well. The contract would then be in danger of cancellation or unfavorable revision.

The truth was that the sensitivity and accuracy of the original tracker design had always been less than the best. The experimental unit was a bit of a fluke. Even so, it didn't quite meet the specification for which Trackers Unlimited had contracted. New optical systems analysis predicted success, as long as a lot of tolerances were met, so with luck the new design might work swimmingly and meet most objectives. Time was the immediate problem. The prototype star tracker was to be delivered to the Navy in only three months. The contract plan was to have the tracker undergo several weeks of sea trials aboard a naval electronics auxiliary vessel, the *U.S.S. Compass Island*.

Detailed design takes time. Precision machining takes time. Assembling and testing finicky electro-optical gear often takes the most time of all. The remaining time before the required delivery was just about enough to complete design, fabrication, and assembly of the system. Work went on, but there were the usual surprises waiting for the star tracker builders. As a result, the tracker was completely assembled for the first time only days before delivery was to take place. The engineers were doing their best, but the system wasn't responding well. The dimensions of the optics were slightly off. The gimbals were not quite right. The motor drive was sticky. This system was supposed to track a daytime star. But this was not likely without a lot of additional work.

Trackers Unlimited management looked for an easy way out. The old test results were still available, and could be used with some vague wording to qualify the new tracker system for delivery. This would be a little phony, but the systems were somewhat similar and the numbers were real. The tests used for qualification just wouldn't be done on the system to be delivered. A management decision was required. To ship or not to ship? That was the question. Whether it would be nobler to accept the slings and arrows of the U.S. Navy by withholding shipment, or to deliver and thereby create a sea of troubles for the field technicians.

During the redesign and assembly work, the technicians had been studying drawings of the old tracker configuration. Normally, they would have been working alongside manufacturing people learning the system, but the gag order was in effect. Marked-up drawings and test sequences for the new system would be made available to the technicians only with the delivery of the hardware. Management said in justification, "These are experienced people who have worked things out for themselves before."

As the delivery time drew near, the president chaired a review of the contract status. The new tracker had been assembled but still not tested. The field technicians would probably have a few weeks of grace to muddle around after the system was delivered. The engineers at the factory were beginning the assembly of a second system that had a much better chance of working than the first one. If things went really sour with the first one, the second might be ready in time to save the day. What the hell, ship the tracker!

The scene shifts to the *U.S.S. Compass Island*. Several boxes have just arrived containing the star tracker, associated electronics, and test equipment, accompanied by two Trackers Unlimited field technicians. Captain Dane met the technicians in the wardroom. The captain, having dealt with new exotic equipment and their masters many times over, asked for an assessment of the state of the gear. The senior field technician, who knew nothing but the company party line, told the captain in all honesty that as far as he knew the equipment had met the full test sequence prior to leaving the plant. Therefore, it should have been a simple matter of setting up the tracker system and running some confirmation tests to prove the already-tested performance.

Captain Dane responded with a welcome aboard speech that was short and to the point. The ship was scheduled to go to Bermuda in five days, and Captain Dane and his crew were very much looking forward to a sojourn in the Caribbean—it was December in Brooklyn. However, before they could go, the tracker must successfully track a daytime star. Failure to do so in the brief time allotted would delay the sailing date by no more than one week. If things were not well by the end of the twelfth day hence, the Trackers Unlimited star tracker, the Trackers Unlimited field technicians, and Trackers Unlimited itself would be gone from the *U.S.S. Compass Island*.

Armed with this vote of confidence, the field technicians set to work. Optics and adjunct electronics were quickly installed topside. The next day, the test equipment was fastened down in the bowels of the ship, and cables were run to the tracker assembly. On the third day, the equipment was turned on. No fuses blew, and no smoke appeared. Everything was going well, so far, but the overhead was about to cave in. It was much like the Steve McQueen story about the man who had just fallen from the 67th floor of his office building. As he fell past the 32nd floor, he heard a concerned voice asking if he was all right, to which the falling man responded, "So far, so good."

On the fourth day, the Trackers Unlimited technicians pointed the tracker at a bright star. No acquisition, no return. Since the moon was visible, they tried pointing to it, checking the pointing angles for correctness as best they could. Still no luck. The captain, who had been watching the proceedings with interest, asked how things were going. Not wanting to cast undue alarm, the response was "So far, so good."

The next day they tried for the sun. It's difficult to miss the sun, but the tracker managed it. The senior field technician called the plant, asking to speak to the responsible engineer on the tracker system. The conversation went something like this:

Technician: "Hi, this is Aldo, aboard the *U.S.S. Compass Island.* We're installing the new tracker, but we don't seem to be able to acquire star, moon, or sun with it. Everything we check seems to be in order. It seems to be pointing correctly. The electronics check out. What can we be doing wrong?"

Engineer: "Gee. I don't know for sure. We never had a chance to test it before it was shipped."

Technician: "What, say?"

Engineer: "The big boss said, "Ship it," just as we were installing it in the test fixture. We don't know if it has a prayer of working. I guess you guys are on your own for now. We can come to the Navy Yard in three or four weeks to give you a hand. By that time, we hope to have a second system available that has a fair chance of working. Better yet, you can ship the whole thing back here, so we can do the job right."

Technician: "What kind of an outfit are we working for? We've got the ship's captain crawling all over us. He is hot to go to Bermuda, but won't leave until the tracker can track a daytime star, or we're off the ship, whichever comes first. We can't tell him the tracker was not tested in the factory. That will be the end of any work Trackers Unlimited ever does for the Navy. On the other hand, we had better show some progress quick, or come up with a real good cover story. What do you suggest?"

Engineer: "Beats me. You might try pointing a flashlight in the telescope and measuring the response. That should tell us something. As for coming up with a story that holds water, your imagination is as good as mine. Be sure and call if we can be of more help. Goodbye and good luck!"

Technician: "What?!"

The United States Navy didn't become the world's best Navy by quietly accepting every little thing their contractors tell them. Captain Dane knew star tracking wasn't easy. If a star tracker system could not find the moon, it was not likely to be able to track a daytime star without some important changes. Important changes took time. He wanted to be on his way to the land of the tan, and soon.

DILBERT reprinted by permission of United Feature Syndicate, Inc.

Back at the tracker, the field technicians decided to take the advice offered them. They found a big flashlight. The junior field technician headed topside with the flashlight while Aldo went below. Once below decks, Aldo reconnected the microphones and headset. As soon as the two technicians were able to communicate, Aldo had his colleague put the flashlight about six inches from the tracker lens and turn it on. Aldo spoke first.

Aldo: "Is the flashlight on?"

Junior: "Sure is. What do you see on the scope?"

Aldo: "Not a thing! Wave it around."

Junior: "It's waving."

Aldo: "Turn the flashlight off and then on, and keep doing it until I tell you to stop."

Junior: "I've turned the light on and off about a hundred times. Can I stop now?"

Aldo: "Might as well. There's nothing doing. We have a problem."

Captain Dane, who had walked in quietly behind Aldo and witnessed the proceedings, asked coldly, "Do you really think that you can get this thing to track a daytime star this year, when so far, you haven't been able to find a very bright flashlight six inches in front of the telescope? I am looking for results, and they don't seem to be forthcoming. Therefore, unless you can convince me that at some point in the recent past, this equipment worked, and that you have a very good handle on your problems, and that whatever these problems are, they are easily fixed, I will have the crew pack up the Trackers Unlimited equipment and remove it *and* you from my ship immediately. How about it?" All Aldo could do was stammer that it appeared there may have been some shipment damage, but he didn't know what it was.

The Trackers Unlimited technicians and their gear left the ship as soon as the tracker equipment could be put back into the crates. The *U.S.S. Compass Island* left for the Caribbean on the following night. A few days later, after a private conference with his manager, Aldo quit. Meanwhile, the star tracker contract was reviewed, renegotiated, and finally canceled.

There is no defense for the behavior of Trackers Unlimited top management. They gambled and lost. Would the truth have helped? Probably. Tracking stars requires the use of very precise electro-optical equipment. Trackers Unlimited had shown that it knew how to go about building such equipment, but had problems with the execution. The Navy needed the product. They needed it badly. No one else had anything better. The chances were very good that the Navy, after giving Trackers Unlimited management a good tongue-lashing, would have continued to support the project. With the second system about to be evaluated, Trackers Unlimited had a good ace in the hole, but once caught up in the lie, their credibility with the Navy was near zero.

Union Suit

Among the least sought engineering management tasks is one of directly dealing with bargaining unit representatives. Union representatives seem to enjoy giving management trouble, and some are past masters with the needle. Some years ago, *21-UC10*, an infamous ruling of the National Labor Relations Board (NLRB), was born. Essentially, this ruling decreed that, unless already union members, people in engineering development laboratories doing work covered elsewhere in a contract with the bargaining unit were infringing upon union rights. Up to that time, engineering technicians were considered to be exempt employees even though they often did the same work as manufacturing technicians. The difference was that the engineering technicians worked from sketches, verbal instructions, and imagination rather than from released drawings. Arguments that this difference was important and real carried no weight with the NLRB.

Implementation of *21-UC10* was painful. Engineering technicians typically wanted no part of a union, yet if they wanted to continue to work under the watchful eyes of the union stewards, they would have to join the bargaining unit. Engineers who had been used to hands-on development now had to work through a second pair of union hands. Even the act of carrying a scope probe across the lab by a non-union person was taken as cause for a grievance. Engineering supervisors were inundated with union grievances.

As bad as the situation was, it was made worse by some managers who would routinely and deliberately lie about the characteristics of a job being performed by a non-union technician. In order to stop this spate of trouble and ill will, top management and the NLRB simply transferred most of the engineering technicians into the union. This act set up a howl throughout engineering group. Several engineering managers fired the technicians as soon as they were transferred into the union (through no fault of their own). These managers then closed their laboratories to union representatives under the guise of security. These acts brought an immediate response from the union demanding laboratory access under the threat of a plant strike, and it based its claim on the company's "bad faith bargaining." The union representatives were soon granted access, and it immediately filed grievances against any technician who touched laboratory equipment. Some technicians were hired back as union members, but the grievances continued unabated.

Laboratory work had to be done. The company couldn't keep paying grievance money at the rate they were losing grievance decisions, so driven by engineering management to do something, the personnel department established a new non-union advanced technical payroll (ATP) for the more experienced technicians. The hope was that these people would be doing work requiring original thought, and the union would back off. To make things more believable, the personnel department found some recently laid off ex-engineers and hired them.

The lies on both sides burgeoned. As technicians who had been in the union only a short time were "promoted" into this payroll and out of the union, the union leaders howled. They encouraged their members and representatives to file grievances under any pretext. Management would simply deny the grievances at the first level, regardless the merits of the complaints. At this point, both management and union positions had hardened. There was no give and take. As hard-line union members with plenty of seniority replaced the less senior technicians, a few acts of sabotage occurred. The newly created ATP classification was becoming more troublesome. The ATP idea had been put together in haste to satisfy engineering managers, but now these same managers were finding that the line between an ATP and an engineer was blurring. Over time, virtually all the ATPs understandably wanted to be reclassified as engineers, but when they were rebuffed, they often quit or filed their own grievances with the company.

The problems became fewer over time, but they never went away completely. Before, mutual respect characterized the engineer-technician relationship, now distrust was common. The quality of laboratory output suffered. Engineers couldn't appear to be taking test data, so often they didn't review the results with care. Test setups were constructed less carefully than before. Engineering laboratories took on the aura of a more formal manufacturing area with paper passing between the engineer and the technician when previously there had been personal contact.

The *21-UC10* decision was probably politically motivated, and was poorly thought out. The position hardening that never went away was **due to a breakdown in communication** between engineering management and the union leaders caused by the telling of lies, both by company management and by union members. The ultimate goals of both sides were the same—more sales and more jobs. But with the initial falsehoods, the little mutual respect they once held for each other evaporated, never to return.

CHAPTER 8

Takeover

"O generation of vipers."
– Matthew 3:7

IF STRUCK BY A BUYOUT, merger, or reorganization, stay calm and keep a low profile until things shake out, but keep a current resumé at hand.

In this day and age, it's likely that a manager will have some personal involvement in a merger, takeover, or major company restructuring. These trauma-producing changes create risks for virtually everyone involved, but they also offer opportunities as well. Perhaps the more gut-wrenching consequences of corporate upheaval come after the purchase of the company when the new owners are looking to turn pieces of their acquisition into ready cash. But even being on the buying end of a deal has its risks.

Most moderately successful, publicly traded corporations are intermittently being evaluated for sale, merger, or takeover, whether the mid-level company management knows it or not. Top managers have a somewhat better view of these machinations, but they too are often surprised when a hostile takeover group emerges. Most deal makers prudently don't talk much until the deal comes together. Behind the scenes, there are people who spend a lot of time fending off or investigating the worth of potential deals. When a deal is finally closed, all involved find themselves facing a set of unknowns and possibly a hostile environment. Even so, **there are some proven things to do to minimize the uncertainties and maximize the potential that comes along with this involuntary chaos.**

Having more or less successfully survived a major buyout and two takeovers, I believe the best course of action is to strike a low profile until the power players are well identified and the logic (if any) behind the new structure becomes apparent. Whether bought or sold, this change is a harbinger of trying times. **When two companies combine, there are always winning and losing factions. One is not a *de facto* winner just because one was part of the surviving entity. People from either side may well get the upper hand.**

Make no mistake, many top managers are as frightened and unsure as lower-level managers, but they know more about the players and the boundary conditions than the others do. Hence, top management tends to fare somewhat better. I've observed that **a few months after the change, more than two-thirds of the buying company's management survived, and the bought-out company had a survival rate of a little more than one-half.** The mix of survivors a year after the combination is far less certain, but will almost surely include managers brought in from the outside to shore up perceived internal management weaknesses. Typically, these new people will gain the upper hand for about a year until they are proven to be no better or worse than the managers who were initially suspect.

The most common reason given for combining organizations is that the same work can be done with fewer people. Those at the top believe that this efficiency improvement is preordained and will act accordingly. A tendency of surviving top managers is to look at the middle management structure with a jaundiced eye and to do away with more of these managers than reason would dictate. For strange and unclear reasons, non-middle management typically presumes that middle managers do less useful work for their rate of pay than other employees do.

Heads will surely roll, but these remorseless acts also serve to remove some of the competition for the better jobs, making it a little easier for the survivors to recover as things zigzag back to normal. For those whose heads are removed from the organization chart, they should not despair. Those first affected have the first opportunity to apply for the better openings in the area. The second wave will probably find the pickings leaner.

It is good to take full advantage of all of the offers made by the company to ease the termination blow, even if one feels to have been dealt with unfairly and wants nothing more than to leave the den of thieves. The surviving management isn't likely to be crestfallen by a refusal to accept what they offer. It was probably done for public relations purposes anyway. It can't hurt to ask for even more than is offered. With things in a state of flux, the human resources people may be willing to grant requests to subsidize telephone, travel, and other expenses the terminated (or soon-to-be terminated) manager will incur while searching for other employment.

Those who remain after the first wave goes should not become complacent and think that the danger has passed. It has not. At this point, no one knows how the organizations will mesh. It is not uncommon for the revised company to go through three waves of management before things stabilize. The following illustrative story made the rounds a few years ago.

It seems that a manager found himself replacing a colleague who had been caught in the first wave of staff reductions after a company buyout. As the departing manager bid farewell, he gave his friend three numbered envelopes with instructions to open number one and heed the advice therein the first time he felt seriously threatened by the new management. The second and the third envelopes were to be opened in order and read if things went sour a second or third time.

In short order, the new manager was called to account for the poor schedule performance plaguing his organization. Prior to a command meeting with the president, he opened the first envelope. The message in the envelope read, "Blame the problems on prior management." As the president seemed to be preparing to dismiss him for his schedule short-comings, our manager observed that things had been in such a mess before he took over that even though there were now several very positive changes in place, the full effect hadn't been felt yet. The president thought a bit, and said, "Perhaps you haven't been given sufficient time to correct the sins of your predecessors." The new manager went back to work, thanking his friend and breathing a sigh of relief.

In the following months, schedule performance had improved marginally but product costs were now getting out of hand. Once again he was in trouble. He opened the second envelope. The note inside contained a single word, "Reorganize." During the next meeting with the president, he pointed out how costs were driven up by the vagaries of the existing organization. Therefore, significant cost improvements could be achieved by reorganizing. He presented a plan to do just that. The president agreed that a reorganization was probably needed. The reorganization plan was accepted.

A couple of months later, with schedules and costs both turning sour, he was once again preparing to confront the president. He opened the third envelope. It read, "Prepare three envelopes."

In a buyout or takeover, clear-thinking managers should ask subordinate managers to interview and make preliminary evaluations of the employees in their respective organizations. These employees are unknowns for the new manager, and these evaluations are extremely important. **First evaluations set the tone of the manager-employee relationship for some time to come.**

A subordinate should not try to force a relationship with the new manager. The new manager should initiate the first contact, hopefully after having read all the positive things that may already be in the personnel folders. **Scheduling meetings and discussions with the new boss at this point tends to be counterproductive.** Any requests should be made very care-fully and should always deal with important business issues. The new manager is very busy at this juncture learning about people and absorbing the purpose of the organization, while trying to manage day-to-day operations. This probably requires working and reading late into the night. Any discussions that do not address issues the new manager considers timely and vital are likely to be cut short. Even a new manager would rather spend time relaxing with family and friends than be in nonessential meetings. In other words, do not irritate your manager.

Go West, Old Men

In this next tale, those who expected to be the winners turned out to be the losers.

The raiders from Texas adjusted their eye patches, then checked their guns and sabers. They were preparing to turn a stunning defeat into victory by pillaging a part of the Southern California aerospace civilization. Some months before the attack, the raiders had been on the wrong end of a corporate takeover. Their large, diverse communication and electronics firm had been losing money for some time. They were bought by a cash-rich, no-nonsense company with significant aerospace holdings in California. Portions of this company's already-existing California businesses complemented the Texans' activities; hence, mergers of several subordinate organizations ruled the day.

The Californians were in trouble, too. Some time back they had "won" an Air Force contract to provide navigation and flight control systems for a new multipurpose fighter-bomber. The contract was fixed-price and incentive-based, and the product was behind schedule, over cost, and didn't work very well. Although, as one senior Air Force procurement officer observed, "If you can fix any one of those three problems, you would be the best supplier I have!" The parent company was digging into the corporate coffers to pay for these overruns. Any future offsetting program incentives were unlikely to be justified, and in any case, the maximum possible incentives wouldn't be a patch on the losses incurred to date. The company's corporate managers were understandably cranky about the California performance. Furthermore, the top managers had been living with the California troubles for some time, so they knew them in detail. The Texans' problems were still new to them and had only been viewed from afar, so the management performance of the Texans looked far better to the corporate fathers than that of the Californians.

The Texans had considerable recent experience in sweeping problems away by blaming them on circumstances beyond anyone's control, prior management, poor organization, or just bad luck. The Californians would learn from the Texans and refine these techniques as time went on, but at first, they were not nearly as adept. Most of the troubles at both sites stemmed from the same source; underbidding military contracts to capture new business. Neither the Texans nor the Californians had sufficient experience with fixed-price contracts to keep themselves out of trouble. Nevertheless, the corporate hierarchy had finally decided that as new organizations were formed from the prior pieces, the Texans were to be put in charge. It was not a good time to be from California.

Various management functions moved to Texas. Anyone from California who was asked to relocate to Texas, and didn't, was out. Past successes meant nothing. The Californians remaining in California were expected to embrace Texas vernacular and Texas style. Failure to do so was a ticket to oblivion.

Non-managers fared somewhat better. There was still a lot of work to be done, and people were needed to do it. Most operators, engineers, and scientists were retained whether or not they could speak Texan. **Managers who wanted to stay with the company opted out of management, believing correctly that when the boat quit rocking, they might be allowed to manage again.** Meanwhile, a lot of good employees left, voluntarily or otherwise, for more compatible surroundings.

Just as one can't pick relatives, one can't pick a manager gained in a takeover. If the new manager is odd, options are limited, but for a while, at least, a reasonable course of action is to try to make the best of it. It is quite likely that a really bad actor will be found out before long. One of the more interesting general managers who came with the Texas takeover was a man who was a closet alcoholic and somewhat of a sexist. His demeanor appeared highly unusual to the Californians. Somehow (up to that time) most had been spared contact with his sort. They never knew where they stood with him. Sometimes this man appeared personable and reasonable. On more than one occasion, though, he had gone out of his way to compliment a Californian, only to fire that person the following day.

He picked two new vice presidents based on his perception of their ability to drink like gentlemen. He had a huge staff composed of ex-managers from Texas who, in the past, had shown their inability to manage. This staff created trouble by espousing simplistic solutions to complex problems. They listened and reported half-truths to the Texas management, until the Californians learned to give them lip service and stay out of their way. As the organization floundered, this curious executive came under more and more scrutiny. He was finally removed. It was a pity that it took the better part of two years to get him out of harm's way.

Competent incoming managers will find time to learn about their new employees. **Examining personnel files is usually an effective way to digest pertinent information about the new, if temporary, directly reporting managers.** Some Texans, however, added a new twist. They edited and removed items in the folders that they reviewed. This was apparently based on the idea that all Californians were suspect. Hence, anything conflicting with the new manager's notions of the qualities of the taken over was removed from the personnel folders. Many favorable career histories were wiped out.

Fortunately, selective editing of personal history appears to be a relatively rare occurrence in American businesses, but it does happen. There is really no good defense against this heinous practice. People in charge can do pretty much what they want, and the subordinate may never know. Remembering that the first new boss in the takeover may well not be the last, **a measure of protection can be derived by maintaining a complete personal history file separate from the one kept by the company.** This file can be a great aid, not only during takeovers, but also when changing jobs, which is quite possible under the circumstances. Such documentation will also be invaluable if a lawsuit is initiated by either company or employee.

In addition to using unusual management selection criteria, the Texans had a penchant for hiring consultants to help manage themselves and the renegade Californians. One of the stranger consultants was a self-styled and rather arrogant computer consultant who did not have a great deal to be arrogant about. He had a vision that his favorite programming language called CP/M would be the language of choice for the next hundred years or so, as soon as people came to their senses. That CP/M would be universally embraced was neither reasonable nor possible, but the Texas management knew little of programming. They went along, directing the programming staff to switch from whatever language they were using to CP/M. Fortunately, the programmers worked in a world of their own, and continued to promote and use the languages they knew, principally C. Today CP/M is an anachronism.

One of the poorer characteristics of the takeover management was the lack of follow up to determine the effects of the direction they had given. Quite often, they would forget their prior direction completely, giving conflicting orders from visit to visit. This forgetting became so common that detailed direction from Texas was disregarded in California. If the financial results appeared acceptable, anything bad was forgotten, if not forgiven. If the financial results were bad, anything good was ignored.

Physically remote divisions of a large company can limp along on auto-pilot and inertia for some time before corporate management senses a disturbing trend. It took about a year and a half and a series of worsening financial results for corporate management to realize the Texans weren't superheroes, even though they could talk without moving their lips. So it was decided that neither the Texans nor the Californians were to be trusted. The senior bosses now initiated the second phase, that of recruiting and hiring outside talent to run the businesses. As a result, new people were hired at various management levels, and they brought their friends with them. These friends initially showed up as consultants, ostensibly to advise the new bosses. They were everywhere, collecting and evaluating information about the day-to-day running of the businesses. Unbeknownst to the existing managers, most of these consultants were slated to become directors and senior executives. Sad was the manager who spoke openly and honestly with these people during the fact-finding sessions. Sad were those managers who in times past had rubbed their colleagues the wrong way. They were maligned at will behind their backs, sometimes to their prospective bosses masquerading as consultants. As with any group of people, some of these consultants were good, and some were bad. In retrospect, it seems that those who were bad were good and bad. In any event, it is always dangerous to take a consultant at face value.

A word to prospective takeover management. It is not a good idea to bring in outside managers in large groups, or at more than one level at a time, regardless of the presumed incompetence of the existing management. Results can become rapidly worse when saddled with several new reporting managers, who are unknown to the workers and to each other.

Both the California and Texas divisions under the new managers were now even less able than before to focus on real problems. This diversion of attention did little for profitability. Meanwhile, a lot of the new managers were spending time in turf struggles and trying to sort out how the parent corporation really operated.

In addition to the error of hiring new managers in droves, corporate management blundered further. The new executives had been promised near autonomy during their interviews; however, corporate management did not really intend to allow it. It never occurred to them that the newly hired managers might take them seriously. Unfortunately, the new managers believed they had the right to remake their respective organizations in their own image. As they tried, corporate managers were appalled, and they quickly took steps to rein in these new managers. Disillusion quickly set in among the newly hired managers. This disillusion caused more dissension in the managerial ranks. Some of the new managers left within the first three months of their employment. Others stayed longer but never could get it right.

After a couple more years and uncounted millions of dollars lost, the corporate management decided to try again. By this time, most of the newer managers had quit. A few of the new guard and a lot of the old guard were trying to run the show from mostly acting positions. Qualified replacement managers were hard to come by. As the new wave of managers quit, they put the word out to industry. Worse yet, corporate management no longer trusted anyone, so they ruled that corporate staff should confirm all new managers and all significant managerial promotions in these divisions. The corporate staff lacked understanding of the divisions' needs, and because they were separated from these divisions by two thousand miles, they felt little urgency to act. Consequently, only a few of the badly needed replacements were made. The stage was now set for the next debacle.

One thing to be said about this company's corporate managers—they had staying power. Lesser (or perhaps more rational) people would have cut their losses and sold, merged, or closed several of the divisions after the second round of problems surfaced. The third time, they got part of it right. In one division, they decided to hire only a general manager, and they gave him some real authority. Unfortunately, even though change should begin at the top, it is still possible to form a divisive organization when the wrong person is leading it.

The new general manager had a fair number of hangers-on that he had acquired over the years. For a second time, the existing managers were exposed to fact-finding consultants. They remembered what had happened the last time. They knew now to watch their words and their backs. They knew that at least some of the consultants would end up replacing some of them. Underground organization charts were drawn with the most likely consultants put into the most likely management positions.

One member of this group of consultants was a bombastic marketing man who had been out of touch with the industry for some time, but who had both ears of the new general manager. This marketing man's style brought out the worst in people. He held interminable question and answer sessions with the existing management. His cover story was that he was evaluating the product line. He fooled no one. All of the interviewees knew his real objective was to evaluate the management before he took over. He would try to goad unsuspecting managers into blurting raw thoughts they would be sorry for later. He enjoyed what he was doing, and he was a difficult person to like. In due course, he became the new marketing director.

The existing managers had to decide once again whether to leave, or to stay and keep the proverbial low profile. More stayed than left, but a few of those who stayed violated the low profile principle. They tried to influence the actions of the new general manager and his band of ex-consultants by giving them unsolicited aid and succor. These managers soon found themselves on the outside. The rest hunkered down further. Enough fear and uncertainty were going around that even good managers were laying traps one for another. Such backbiting and double-dealing had rarely been seen since the days of the Third Reich. The sales and profit forecasts were fantasy. The financial results were miserable. Everyone but the holdover management held the credibility of holdover management in serious question. The new people were determined to chastise the old for presumed past sins while working side-by-side with them. Staff meetings were much like sessions of the British House of Commons, with invective spewing over those assembled, by those assembled. The general manager encouraged his subordinate managers to embarrass each other, forgetting for the moment that there was a division he was responsible for that was in serious trouble. The yowling, spitting, and clawing weren't helping.

It isn't easy, even in retrospect, to find much rational thought behind all these goings on. It soon became apparent that even though the general manager was trying his best to appear decisive, he wasn't. When he was hired, he told corporate management that he would be a new broom. He promised to clean house in a big way. He was under pressure to get rid of as many of the existing managers as possible, but he didn't want to be personally involved. So he encouraged his newly hired managers to make things so uncomfortable for the old that many of them would leave of their own accord. This notion didn't work at all well. The few that quit or retired were the better managers. As these people left, the vacancies remained unfilled. It seems that even cronyism has its limits where self-preservation is concerned. Once again, it was impossible to hire or transfer anyone of perception into such an organization. Some of the first and second wave of managers lashed back, giving the new managers pause. Many of the third wave of managers began to fear decision making. They knew they would be challenged, and no one in the division wanted to be found wrong. The division drifted, losing opportunity and then more opportunity. The unusual management philosophy of this leader cost the parent company more than they will ever know.

Only after the general manager left for greener pastures did the wounds begin to heal. Most of the managers who came with him left shortly after him. This time, a general manager was found who was a thoughtful and reasonable person. Management sniping and quarreling gradually subsided. New managers were hired and integrated one at a time. Most promotions were made from within. When no internal candidates were available, good people were recruited. The vacant higher-ranking jobs were usually filled first. No consultants were visible. Once again, managers learned to cooperate and began working together to right the ship.

The problems at this and other divisions of the company were strongly influenced by the philosophy governing takeover management selection. There was at first a clash of cultures, then no discernable culture as waves of new managers passed through and out. Had the managerial changes started at the top and had there been fewer and better managers, the second and third waves may have never been needed.

CHAPTER 9

A Computer Is a Tool— Just Like a Hoe

"640 K ought to be enough for anybody."
– T Watson — IBM

AT ONE TIME OR ANOTHER, I have dealt with virtually every form of computer. While the manager's understanding of today's powerful digital equipment is growing daily, this understanding is spotty. There is modest confusion about what these powerful tools can do for, or to, us. Focused management attention on the abilities and limitations of the modern computer is essential if industry and government are to properly use and control this still burgeoning technology.

Let's consider pieces of the computing industry past. In particular, some examples of use and misuse of the computer may serve to remove some of the mystique that still clings to the digital machine.

When people blame their computers for failing to get things right, it causes the hair on the back of my neck to stand up. This sort of criticism typically stems from a lack of understanding, a need to show one's superiority, or a need for a scapegoat, coupled with fear. When things go wrong with their computers, most people don't know what else to do besides reboot, reinstall, or buy a new computer.

Technical people and all managers must appear to be computer-conversant whether or not they know a bit from a byte. I recently learned to my chagrin that prospective mathematics professors can be selected (and deselected) for their perceived knowledge of not only computers but of particular programming languages. It's perplexing because many professorial applicant selections are made by people who themselves are not particularly computer-conversant.

I was fortunate to have been able to work with several of the early interesting machines. I wrote a bit of simple sequential code and punched cards for the first IBM Card Programmed Calculator, then graduated to the Bureau of Standards Western Automatic Computer (SWAC) at UCLA. The SWAC was a research computer in the purest sense. Soon after the SWAC, the IBM 701 took me down a peg. I next programmed what was probably the first ever digital real-time control system. I had a lot of fun working on digital simulations of the Nautilus navigation system (the one that made the first trip under the North Pole). I developed Minuteman I flight and ground programs using an airborne computer with a spinning disk main memory. The entire onboard program for Minuteman I required only 2,560 words. Take that, you megabyte-mad programmers!

The current (at this writing) desktop computer with its 300+ megahertz clock rates, its 6+ gigabyte hard disk storage, and its many, many megabyte internal semiconductor memory is a far cry from the earliest digital machines. Those old computers were big and bulky, gulped power, and overheated the environment. No matter, today's computers have the identical basic internal functions of the early digital computers. They all have, and always have had, binary innards. The language of all digital computers is the language of off-on switches. The computer hardware knows nothing of any alphabet or the decimal number system, and what's more, it doesn't care.

The earliest of the stored program machines wasn't all that early. Probably the first to operate was the very secret (at the time) British "Colossus II" in June 1944. This was a machine using some 2500 valves (British for vacuum tubes) designed specifically to rapidly decipher German code patterns derived from an updated "Enigma" machine having several more coding wheels and detents than the original three-wheeled Enigma. Meanwhile, by 1945 John von Neumann had outlined the architecture for the modern digital computer in his now famous First Draft of a Report on the EDVAC. The first truly general-purpose machines, the EDVAC (Electronic Discrete Variable Automatic Computer), the ENIAC (Electronic Numerical Integrator and Computer), and the EDSAC (Electronic Delay Storage Automatic Computer) were all based on von Neumann's work. The ENIAC was more or less complete circa 1946. (The EDSAC has often been credited with being the first operating stored-program computer.) EDSAC was completed in 1949 by a group headed by M. V. Wilkes at Cambridge University in England. A bit later, this same group was the first to write and use programs intended to make the work of programmers easier, possibly because Wilkes found early on how easy it was to make programming errors.

Before the programming aids came along, the only way to create a new stored program was to laboriously fashion an extensive pattern of binary digits that meant something to both the person and the machine. This huge binary pattern was then entered sequentially into the computer, digit by digit, using toggle switches. By 1950, the people flipping switches were replaced by holes in punched paper, teletype tape, and a slow paper tape reader. Errors made by the switch flippers and the contemporary paper tape readers were about equal.

As soon as they learned of their existence, the scientific community rapidly realized what these computing machines could do for them. They could perform analyses of large data sets that had been virtually impossible to deal with before. Scientists and engineers could now program generally precise and repeatable simulations of a myriad of complex mechanical, chemical, and electrical systems. Earlier simulations were typically had by laboriously making a physical model or creating a program for an analog computer. Analog computers were so-named because they would solve problems by connecting electrical and sometimes mechanical building blocks (analogs of the real things) in a way that purported to represent the real-world system.

An analog computer of the 1950s typically consisted of hundreds of vacuum tube amplifiers hooked together in arcane ways by programming patch boards. The solutions would take the form of scaled continuous voltage or current measurements. Analog computers had two principal flaws. They broke down a lot, and the solutions generally weren't repeatable. These computers came into being because it was usually cheaper and easier to set them up than to build a physical model of a chemical plant or to create a model to simulate production line flow. In spite of their shortcomings, these computers proved very useful then, and at the time, there was nothing better. Today, derivatives of the old analog computer have found their way into functional subsystems like antilock brake controllers and CD players. A few fairly complex analog computing systems are still around, mostly married to digital computers and used in specialized applications like flight simulators.

In the 1940s, the Naval Research Laboratory (NRL) marched to a different drum. They decided to go for a computer made up of relays instead of hot and unreliable vacuum tubes. (About the same time the Watson Scientific Computing Laboratory at Columbia University was also working on relay machines.) Relays are natural elements for binary machines, but the clattering of thousands of relays must have been nerve wracking, and the reliability of relays was no better than that of vacuum tubes. The NRL machine maintenance was so difficult, that for a time, as the story goes, there was only one man who could successfully repair the monster. Understandably, he had a drinking problem.

IBM is a pretty savvy outfit. Early on, they set out to satisfy the calculating and computing requirements of the business world. After all, "Business" is IBM's middle name. IBM introduced the card-programmed calculator in the 1940s. Slow and noisy, it was still a big improvement over the hand-cranked (later motorized) desk calculator and the ugly comptometer. The permanent memories of these IBM machines were literally the punched cards that were later used everywhere for computer input and output.

It was the data limitation of the IBM card format that gave rise to the use of only the last two digits to identify the current year. This ambiguity has now manifested itself as the "millennium bug problem," whose potential impact has been nicely overstated by the media. I don't question that a lot of money and other resources can be expended fixing the bug problem. I only question the need for most of the effort.

During this early period, computers operated with near-glacial slowness. A major limiting factor was the speed of the memory elements. High (even medium speed) memories were not around yet. Magnetic drums were just becoming available for central memories, but they allowed access to information only in selected sequential strings. These memories were slow and quite unwieldy by modern standards. If the information needed from a drum memory didn't happen to be rotating under a fixed-read head, everything stopped until it was.

Random access memories (RAMs) were being developed in several laboratories, but wouldn't be available commercially until about 1955. A RAM permits a processor to read from, or write into, any part of the memory with a single small fixed delay, eliminating the variable penalty, or latency, of rotating drums, disks, tapes, and the like. Magnetic core RAM memories were on the horizon but had several problems precluding their early acceptance. Once in use, they would be always limited to one bit of memory per core, requiring a tremendous number of cores.

Enter Professor Williams from England. He and his team had succeeded in using, of all things, a cathode ray tube (CRT) as an internal high-speed memory. This memory idea had been used a little earlier in computers like the SWAC. The SWAC's CRT memory bank was composed of some thirty-six CRTs. The size of the SWAC's internal memory was a whole thirty-two words, each one, thirty-six bits long. One bit from each of the thirty-two words was stored in each tube. Data reliability was a serious problem. The SWAC internal memory exhibited three stable states: a 1, a 0, and a maybe. In these memories, the stored 1s and 0s lasted only briefly as electric charges in the phosphor on the tube face. Before the information could fade away, sensing circuitry detected their presence by first writing all 1s into the CRT and destroying all the 0s. The spots where there used to be 0s would show a little voltage blip when they were changed into 1s.

The voltage associated with the 1 spots wouldn't change. Most of the time, 0s were then written back in the spots where they belonged.

Williams' Tubes worked somewhat better than the earlier SWAC memory. After some tests and negotiation, Williams' Tube memories were bought by IBM for the early 700 series computers. These machines were fast for the day but were error prone, mostly because of the memory glitches. Despite these errors, IBM sold and leased a lot of 701s.

Early in the production cycle of the 701, T. Watson, the big-big gun at IBM at the time, held a testimonial dinner for Professor Williams. At the time, the legendary IBM motto "THINK" was displayed everywhere. It was seen in IBM elevators and hallways, in managers' offices, and at back of the dining hall where the dinner was held. During dessert, Mr. T. Watson formally asked Professor Williams to describe how his team came up with such an innovative solution to the vexing memory problem. Professor Williams, an irascible individual, stared for a moment at the large sign at the back of the hall and said, "Well, we didn't just sit about thinking, you know, we went out and actually did something!" To my knowledge, IBM never purchased anything again from the Williams group.

About this time, business-oriented people working with card-programmed calculators and small IBM 650 drum memory machines looked at what the scientists were doing and said, "We'll have some of that." They didn't have much use for simulations and for solving complex differential equations, but they wanted to crunch a lot of numbers fast. They particularly liked the idea of creating massive programs once, and then turning the computers loose on month-end closings, inventories, pay check preparation, and similar tasks. What they didn't like was that research or engineering groups controlled the big computers, and that the programming of these machines took skills that at the time were rare in the business world. But in short order, the financial departments of most large companies convinced top management that these big expensive computers were now being used by several functions and that computer time would be better used if computing were under the wing of business people rather than the profligate engineers. The concept of central computing was born.

Program development cost and schedule problems began to plague the financial community. In an attempt to ease this burden, a programming language tailored to business applications was developed. It was called COBOL (Common Business Oriented Language). COBOL persists in a few out of the way places to this very day. Meanwhile, back in the research and engineering groups, a cult of machine-language programmers was forming. It seems ludicrous today but the impetus was the fear lost jobs if programming languages were allowed to ease the programmers' workload. (The few of us still left who were around at the time fervently believe that life is too short to code more than one program in machine language.) Despite a groundswell of fear, FORTRAN (FORmula TRANslation language) was introduced for use by the scientific community circa 1957. FORTRAN was followed by a host of other high-level languages designed to improve productivity and take a lot of the drudgery out of programming. Hordes of programmers fought the use of these languages tooth and nail. For a while, it was the early Industrial Revolution all over again. Fortunately, these new and powerful languages won hands down, or there wouldn't be enough people in the world to write and check out the programs we commonly use today.

The truly general-purpose computers (mainframes) of the late 1950s and early 1960s were, for the most part, big hulking things. The internal high-speed memories could only hold a piece or two of the needed programs and data. The rest of the information was stored in auxiliary memories until used, and then copied into RAM from which the active instructions were taken. Auxiliary memories were mostly banks of spinning tape reels well known from bad sci-fi flicks. Transistors were coming into general use, but vacuum tubes were still around, creating heat and failing with disturbing regularity. Semiconductor diodes were by contrast fairly common.

In the 1950s, IBM dominated the field of mainframe computers, with the UNIVAC 1100 series being second. Several companies dealing in high-tech endeavors of the time sensed that something big was building and jumped into the fray. Bendix made a hit for a time with the small G-15 and then the larger and faster G-20. Xerox entered a bit later by buying out Bendix Computer. Soon after, Librascope's LGP-30 and North American's RECOMP were offered for sale. These were all relatively modest entries when compared with IBM's 701 or the later 704/709/7090s. The small machines were aimed at the engineering and scientific marketplace as partial replacements for the large capable mainframes that were now centralized. They also found their way into a myriad of real-time control jobs, primarily for the U.S. military. (Big, purely scientific machines were limited to government laboratories, universities, and a think tank or two).

None of these smaller commercial machines sold well. The class of problems they could conveniently deal with were limited, and they typically came with restrictive and relatively poor support and application software. Later DEC's PDP and VAX series computers, Hewlett Packard's 2000s, and a few others made significant, if often temporary, inroads in the middle-ground computer market. The successful manufacturers generally provided good hardware and adequate software.

From the 1960s through the 1980s, the U.S. military represented a huge market for smaller computers, principally those used for real-time control. On-board missile computers, shipboard computers, and field artillery data computers were produced in quantity. For a year or so, North American Aviation's Autonetics Verdan computer had the highest production-run rate of any computer in the free world, exceeding even the run rate of the IBM 650 computer.

By 1963, almost all digital computers used semiconductors freely. Power consumption was down and speed was climbing. Active electrical components were still discrete. Single diodes and single transistors were individually placed and soldered on to circuit boards containing patterns of plated conductors. Integrated circuits had yet to make an appearance. The interconnection of these circuit boards was made by connecting many insulated wires. The inside of a computer was a nightmare, and to some degree, it still is.

Magnetic cores were now available in quantity for central high-speed memories. These cores stored 1s or 0s depending on the direction of the magnetic field in a little toroid made of sintered magnetic material. These memories were still of the destructive readout variety, similar in that respect to the old Williams Tube. The information was destroyed when read and had to be replaced as soon as the sensing electronic logic knew what it was. Any power failure while the central processor was active meant information loss, requiring a restart of the system and a permanent loss of data generated since the last time information was saved to tape. This unfortunate situation hasn't changed much.

During this period, production engineers attacked a plethora of local inefficiencies in the very labor-intensive fabrication of these machines. One of the more interesting cases had to do with the psychology of assembly. The interconnection of something as complex as a computer is not a trivial problem. In one computer assembly plant, wire lengths were measured, pre-cut, pre-soldered, and then binned by length. Initially, the wire insulation for all the wires was white. As time wore on, other insulation colors were used if they were cheaper or just available. When wires of the same length but of more than one color were put into the same bin, wire assembly productivity was dramatically and adversely affected. After some investigation, it was found that the assemblers were trying wires of each color at the points of assembly to see which color combinations they felt to be more aesthetically pleasing, sometimes taking minutes to decide on a wire color before soldering it in. Education and motivational lectures did no good. A return to all wires of the same color in a single bin fixed the problem.

The ballistic missile programs of the late 1950s, 60s, and 70s were a godsend to the development of electronics and to the improvement of component reliability. The Minuteman I ballistic missile was expected to operate continuously on alert for three years without failing. This was a tall order. A big question at the time was whether the availability of such a missile would be better using redundant circuitry, or by spending gobs of money to improve the reliability of the electronic components. Fortunately, management chose the reliability improvement route. These reliability programs gave us the techniques and much of the insight we still use today for fabrication and test of electronics. The resulting reliability of Minuteman I was superb.

The Minuteman II ballistic missile was designed to be a significant change from the Minuteman I. Since the U.S. had in place most of the planned five wings of Minuteman I missiles, the Air Force felt it could take some technical risk in Minuteman II. They decided correctly that a significant savings in weight and assembly complexity would result from using a new technology that allowed a lot of transistors to be placed and connected together on a single silicon die. The first volume use of the integrated circuit (IC) was born, but not without trouble, however. The ICs used today in our computers are virtually all designed in a silicon-based technology called "CMOS" (Complementary Metal Oxide Semiconductor). Minuteman II ICs were bipolar as opposed to the mostly unipolar CMOS. There are two principal functional advantages of CMOS circuits over bipolar circuits for digital applications. One is that CMOS requires much lower average power than bipolar to mechanize digital logic. The second is that CMOS circuits can be made very dense with more function per square anything than bipolar circuitry. However, there was only limited experience with CMOS at the time. Bipolar was a logical technology to use.

In addition to the functional advantages of ICs, analysts predicted a significant improvement in reliability of the ICs over discrete components. The analysts were badly mistaken. The fault lay not in the inherent reliability, but in the device design. Once again, it was found easier to make something worse than to make it better. The Minuteman II bipolar ICs were found to have a built-in failure mode called "latch up." Unwanted, and at the time totally unsuspected, sneak or parasitic current paths caused some switches in these ICs to turn on and stay on until power was shut off. This same problem would affect CMOS today if the device designers didn't constantly guard against it. Unfortunately, radiation from a nuclear blast made the latch up problem worse—not a good quality for a ballistic missile. The solution came from the results of numerous studies followed by a crash redesign of the ICs to isolate internal portions of the circuitry using glass dielectric. The knowledge gained from the Minuteman II program made integrated circuits useful and available to the commercial computer designer soon thereafter.

The early commercial IC designers cut their teeth creating small low-power integrated circuits for hand-held calculators. Initially these circuits were dubbed SSIs (for small scale integration) or MSIs (for medium scale integration). In the 1970s, cutting-edge production facilities were able to achieve one micron (one-millionth of a meter) line widths on 4- or 5-inch diameter silicon wafers. In the late 1990s, the cutting-edge LSI (large scale integration) production lines can achieve less than 0.3 micron line widths on 9-inch silicon wafers with much better yields than twenty years ago. This means that about forty times the number of transistors can be patterned on a single wafer than was possible twenty years ago. These better yields are the driving force for the continual 20 to 25% price reductions of electronics per year and the increase in function per dollar by about the same amount.

With the massive reduction in the cost of components that make up computers (particularly memory), the big mainframes of yesterday have been replaced by the mini-, micro-, and personal computers of today. To be sure, there are still blindingly fast big machines around now that use massively parallel processors to increase computational speeds even further. These computers are connected to workstations and smart terminals that are themselves computers. These stations and terminals are satisfyingly useful in many ways. They can do a lot on their own and they will continue to operate if the central computer goes down. Perhaps most importantly, they provide the means to interactively communicate with the computers of the world. The costs of these tools will probably come down further in real terms, but probably not as fast as in times past. As an example, in 1961, the least expensive internal memory was the rotating magnetic drum. These memories stored data very cheaply for the time. A typical cost was 5 to 10 cents per bit. In late 1997, 16 megabytes (128,000,000 bits) of RAM retailed for about $120.00 or about 0.0001 cents per bit. This dramatic memory cost reduction has been a very important factor in permitting us to put more computing power on our desks today for about a thousand dollars, which is more than a million dollars would have purchased in the late 1950s. **Like the Williams' Tube, the PC semiconductor memory still has volatile storage characteristics and can lose contents when power is interrupted or cut off. Saving to more permanent storage is wise.**

A computer should never be used as a substitute for thought. Make no mistake, a computer does not think. It has the same intelligence as a dull screwdriver. A computer can only sift through complex sets of pre-stored information and arrive at the conclusion that the data indicates and the programmer has ordered. Perhaps later there may be true artificial intelligence, but not now.

It is dangerous to act on any computer-generated information without applying a carefully thought-out reasonableness check. People and computers can make mistakes independently, or more often, together. Several years ago a group of programmers were added to my organization who were developing a dynamic simulation of a ballistic missile from launch to impact. On the first review of the project, it was clear that something was very fishy about the simulation results soon after engine ignition. It seems that the computer program decided that the missile should be going some 1100 feet per second sideways before it had even lifted out of the protective silo. This seemed like very unusual behavior, but no one had noticed. The staff was busily engaged in checking individual subroutines rather than examining the results for reasonableness. The solution was evident to everyone once the problem was pointed out. They were calculating motion relative to the fixed stars and had forgotten the missile was on a rotating earth.

Some time ago, researchers in artificial intelligence at a West Coast university were working on an expert system to help physicians diagnosis and treat various maladies. The method the researchers chose was quite common in the development of artificial intelligence aids. First, they formed a list of illnesses. They then sent out questionnaires containing the list of illnesses to doctors and asked them to list the symptoms, treatments used, and some measure of the effectiveness of these treatments. Flowcharts were then prepared with symptoms as inputs. Identified diseases, treatments, and expected effects of these treatments were the outputs. Inputs and outputs were connected by a set of yes-no switches controlled by a summary of the physicians' answers to the preprogrammed questions. The system had been in modest use for about a year when it was reviewed. One interested reviewer asked how to correct the system when the information it provided was outdated or wrong. He found to his chagrin that the concept of updating or correcting the program was foreign to the system architects. When the reviewer persisted by asking how new diagnostic tools and new treatments were accommodated and incorrect diagnoses and ineffective or dangerous treatments were changed or weeded out, he discovered the architects simply hadn't provided for any of that. That has changed now, but I'm afraid that more than one person has suffered because an educated person didn't think— the computer was supposed to do the thinking.

The universe of computers is still expanding at a rapid rate. At this writing, there are personal computers in over 35% of U.S. homes. New configurations of smaller computers have just arrived on the scene. The laptop computer is everywhere. The handheld PC is a good seller and is quite useful. This little machine can be carried in a jacket pocket, but it is a truly programmable computer capable of communicating with other computers. Several are available using a stripped-down version of Windows.

Recently, there has been a push by a consortium of folks from IBM, Sun Microsystems, and Oracle to return to days of yesteryear where much of the real computing was done on large mainframe computers. The objective of this consortium is to reduce the cost of the local computer. This new/old idea is called network computing. The network computing fan club is working to make an economic case for using these machines in businesses, at least. They are asserting that the low cost of ownership can come from using a fairly capable central machine, coupled through a network to a number of stripped down PC-like computers on desks. The claim is that each PC should cost about $500. The total cost would be quite a bit less than the costs associated with several distributed Pentium PCs doing the same job.

The truth behind any cost comparison is not clear. The $500 estimate for the network computer PC appears suspect, even though a few are being offered now at less than $500. The proponents are likely pricing these machines well below cost to get their feet in the door. Microsoft is critical of these numbers, but it is important to note that Microsoft would be the big loser if the network configuration took off. It is also a bit worrisome that using a network computing system as presently configured would put much of the world's software out of the users' reach.

The world of blindingly fast large processors is still alive and well. Perhaps the cutting edge advances are best exemplified by work at the Lawrence Livermore, Los Alamos, and Sandia National Laboratories. A far-reaching program called ASCI, Accelerated Strategic Computing Initiative, is pushing the state of the art of massive parallel computing. Everything that can be done, or planned, in the name of speed is a part of this effort. The impetus is the requirement for accurate modeling of nuclear weaponry. Mind-boggling new descriptors have come into being. Teraflops (trillions of floating-point operations per second), terabytes (trillions of bytes), petabytes (thousands of trillions of bytes), and exabytes (millions of trillions of bytes) are part of the new vocabulary.

The present plan is to achieve speeds of 100 teraflops by 2004. At this writing, Sandia-Albuquerque has in hand a machine using 9232 Pentium processors computing in parallel and delivering a peak computation rate of 1.8 teraflops. A demonstration at the Lawrence National Laboratories of the final configuration of a 3.2 teraflop machine using 4096 Power 3 processors is planned for late 1998. Equally capable peripherals to feed and accept data from these processors must be developed simultaneously. Algorithms and programming to properly use these capabilities must somehow come to fruition. Directing the analyses, the programming, and the hardware development for such programs will certainly stretch managerial capabilities to the limit.

When computational speed is discussed, the subject of gallium arsenide (GaAs) always rears its head. Processor components made using GaAs are theoretically (and often, actually) faster than those made using silicon, yet GaAs devices are little used. They are expensive. The body of GaAs knowledge and experience doesn't hold a candle to that of silicon-based devices. Arsenic is a poison, so the process of creating the GaAs wafers must be tightly controlled. The quality of the GaAs substrates is generally poorer than that of silicon substrates. GaAs may be the wave of the future, but it always was, and likely always will be.

Pipe Dreams

Tailoring and selecting computer-based systems for use in any business often appears deceptively simple, particularly when seduced by advertising. Selecting systems that will do more good than harm requires knowledge, work, and thought. There is are many choices, but only a few will do the job that management needs. A common solution for smaller businesses is to find and employ a computing consultant to recommend a particular system configuration. Going to an expert is fine; going to an unknown is not. Consider what happened to the owner of Vineyard Pipe.

Not long ago the owner of Vineyard Pipe and Supply Company, an irrigation hardware supplier in a small northern California town, decided to "modernize and computerize." Knowing nothing about computers, he turned to the Yellow Pages for names of firms that might be able to define and configure the right computer system for his business. He contacted a small local computer sales and service house, Golden Byte, and its owner was anxious to help. Soon Golden Byte was under contract to Vineyard Pipe to specify and ultimately supply a computer with matching peripherals and software to be used for inventory monitoring and control and for point-of-sale product identification and pricing.

Golden Byte technicians worked cheaply enough and were worth every penny. They didn't understand the irrigation business but felt they knew computers. A computer was a computer wherever it was used. Golden Byte had put a few customer-unique systems together from pieces it bought from various hardware and software suppliers. It had managed to stay out of court, so far. Fortunately for Golden Byte, its customers didn't expect much. When absolutely necessary, one of the Golden Byte technicians could make a few program modifications to tailor the software to the hardware they had chosen, and to the business at hand.

Having been promised a capable and inexpensive system, the Vineyard Pipe owner left the equipment and software selection entirely up to Golden Byte. A few weeks after the contract signing, the Vineyard Pipe computer system arrived in several boxes. The man from Golden Byte who was supposed to get it all working didn't show up until prodded. When the Golden Byte technician finally arrived, he cabled the pieces together, turned it all on, pronounced the system sound and waved goodbye.

The Vineyard Pipe owner found rather quickly that things weren't going the way the he had hoped. Nothing was straightforward. The manuals were unclear. One or two appeared to have been translated rather hurriedly from Malaysian-Chinese. With the system running well enough to explore some of the functions, Vineyard Pipe found that the programs Golden Byte supplied didn't play well together. A promised product code library was non-existent. At first this didn't matter much since the hardware items in Vineyard Pipe's inventory hadn't yet been labeled. The man from Golden Byte had promised to come back in a week or so to see how things were going and to bring better software. For training support, Golden Byte would later send a different technician to instruct the sales staff how to use the system over a couple of lunch hours.

Vineyard Pipe and Supply was a pleasant old-fashioned hardware store where folks were friendly and relaxed. For years, the pricing policy at Vineyard Pipe had been to price an item when it was entered into inventory and never change it. Customers had a great time looking for the occasional bargain by searching through the bins for the lowest price stickers. The four people working there carried a lot of information in their heads. They generally knew most of the latest prices, and whether or not a requested item was in stock. But as soon as the computer, printer, and scanners were turned on, the owner required his clerks to use the new computer system for all sales. He felt that if the clerks didn't have to use this new flashy system, they wouldn't. His feelings were fully justified.

Included in the late arriving software was a program intended to facilitate the creation of a product library by allowing easy entry of descriptive hardware information, including accompanying UPC data. New labels with UPC codes had to be printed and applied to most everything before point-of-sale scanning would help much. The clerks were now rarely available to help customers. They were tagging inventory. As might be expected, some tags were misprinted and some applied to the wrong items.

When a clerk was pried loose from product tagging long enough to sell something, point-of-sale problems began. As those items with tags were scanned, the program would check to see if sufficient data was in memory to permit it to be priced. Generally there wasn't. The clerk would have to check the price, then go to a set of product catalogs to find the necessary data to feed the computer. Only a fraction of the time would the clerk find everything he was looking for. Even if he found the item in the catalogs, all might not be well. What the computer wanted and what the catalogs supplied were often quite different. The product description format in the computer seemed best suited to a dry goods store. Furthermore, the computer didn't like partial data. When the full product information set wasn't forthcoming, the clerk and the computer were at an impasse. The item simply couldn't be sold using the new system. This required the customer and the clerk to walk over to the owner's office to try for his dispensation to sell the item without having computer approval.

Even when the item to be sold was properly and fully identified, life wasn't a bowl of cherries. The operating system chosen by Golden Byte was of an early single-tasking variety. The invoice printing program didn't like to be timeshared with anything, neither did the scanner. Printing and scanning couldn't be done simultaneously. When items that had been mislabeled were scanned, the customer saw the wrong price. When properly labeled items were misscanned they were mispriced, as well. If the pricing difference wasn't large, it usually went unnoticed, but the inventory count would be in error. When customers were undercharged, they usually didn't say anything. But when they were charged $10.99 for an item fairly priced at $.45, they were understandably miffed. After a few weeks of this kind of treatment, friendly customers became surly.

After fighting the system for a few weeks, the clerks were speaking to the owner only in monosyllables. The most outspoken clerk was summarily fired. Irate customers became sworn enemies of Vineyard Pipe. Calls to Golden Byte, the architects of the disaster, at first went unheeded. They had been fully paid for their work even though it was incomplete. Vineyard Pipe hadn't thought it necessary to provide for warranty and maintenance of the new system.

After several irritable and threatening telephone conversations, extended haggling, and the exchange of more money, Golden Byte agreed to come back to finish what it should have done in the first place. By this time, its lone programmer had quit and no one knew quite what he had done. He had left no documentation of his work. The only descriptive manual available was the one that came with the original code that no longer described the flawed program in use. The owner of Golden Byte was now the sole programmer available. It was up to him to correct and modify somebody else's program. This job was unpleasant. What's more it wasn't one of his more important projects. To make matters worse, he was in similar trouble elsewhere, with more at stake.

For a time, Vineyard Pipe limped along with infrequent and inadequate help from the outfit that got them into trouble. Finally, Vineyard Pipe's owner decided enough was enough, and prepared to issue an ultimatum to Golden Byte. Unfortunately he had waited too long. Golden Byte's telephone wasn't answering. Golden Byte's proprietor had decided to head for Alaska, or maybe it was Australia, and put his troubles behind him.

Vineyard Pipe and Supply was left with a system that frequently crashed, didn't do what it was supposed to do, and was instrumental in alienating employees and customers alike. By this time though, most of the product information had been laboriously entered into the system. Some customers had returned, enticed by price reductions and offers of free services. One of the few things that Golden Byte had done in support of Vineyard Pipe was to finally modify the program to permit partial entry into the computer of inventory data. The point-of-sale terminal was now working most of the time, provided that the clerk didn't scan anything when the printer was printing. Inventory analysis was still a mess, but was being worked on daily by the Vineyard Pipe owner, spurred on by the approach of tax time. The system was poor and unwieldy but had now become a part of the business. It was sure to be replaced if Vineyard Pipe stayed out of bankruptcy.

Vineyard Pipe and Golden Byte must jointly share the blame for what happened. Golden Byte was like many small computer systems and consultation firms spawned by the computer revolution. Competent and experienced computer people should have been alert to at least some of the pitfalls that finished Golden Byte and brought Vineyard Pipe to their knees, but computer specification is a two-way street.

Golden Byte's owner did not plan well. He thought only to configure a system that would perform basic functions that he felt Vineyard Pipe might want. He didn't understand quite what Vineyard Pipe needed, but wasn't too worried since the contract with Vineyard Pipe was rather loose. The computer system was made up of set of components that seemed adequate, given Golden's Byte's limited understanding of the job to be done. The Golden Byte hired hand would go to Vineyard Pipe, open the boxes, cable everything together, install a little modified software, and leave a satisfied customer in his wake.

Vineyard Pipe's owner did not plan at all. He thought he only had to pay money and spend an hour with Golden Byte, describing his business in general terms and letting Golden Byte configure a system to do everything he wanted, all at a fair price, even though he hadn't said explicitly what that was.

Both Golden Byte and Vineyard Pipe would have been better off had they realized that converting a manual system to a computer-centered one is not easy. Whether done manually or by computer, the job functions were no different. Golden Byte should have been given a written summary of the existing business practices at Vineyard Pipe, no matter how simple or primitive. This summary should have included details of the purchasing, accounting, and inventory systems in use; the expected product mix; sales volume; and samples of invoices, sales orders, and other paper used in Vineyard Pipe's business. The Vineyard Pipe owner should have detailed the functions he expected the system to perform now and in the future.

Armed with this information, Golden Byte should have worked up a preliminary system description and implementation plan. The plan should have addressed hardware and software requirements, computer training for Vineyard Pipe employees, and timely on-call support at the Vineyard Pipe store for at least three months after the system was delivered. Once this plan was complete, something approximating the cost of the new system should have been assessed and a bid prepared.

Using the description, plan, and bid as a starting point, Vineyard Pipe and Golden Byte should have met with the goal of mutually understanding the proposed system configuration, the implementation, the effect on the business, and the cost. The owner of Vineyard Pipe would have probably found things left out, wrong, or to his mind, overpriced. At that point, they should have both discussed the trade-offs involved with cost versus function. To get the best or even a good system, Vineyard Pipe should have reviewed the trade-offs. Once they reached an agreement about cost and function, Golden Byte should have written a functional specification for the system at a level the owner of Vineyard Pipe could understand.

I can hear some groans now. "Specification—my God! That will take a year or so to prepare and five years to negotiate. By that time the hardware will be obsolete and we can start over." This is not necessarily so. Such concerns are triggered by the perception that specifications are complex monsters. Specifications need not be monsters; they should be tools that provide a great help to both parties. For a system the size of the one at Vineyard Pipe, four or five pages should suffice. Once the hardware is chosen, only the functions of the system as seen by the user need be addressed. Mentioning things like power and signal characteristics are not important to Vineyard Pipe and needn't be mentioned; however, this information should be contained in the separate hardware specifications. If Golden Byte is concerned, it can monitor local power for a period to decide the types of power conditioners or battery backups Vineyard Pipe should have, and this should be at most one paragraph in the specification.

The nature of the human interaction with the new system is important. It should be well understood and carefully mechanized. The specification should point out any restrictions. How fast is the point-of-sale printer? How much product information can the proposed system hold? Does Vineyard Pipe expect to add more point-of-sale terminals? What about backing up the data? What about graceful degradation if the system fails? What are the provisions for archiving sale and revenue data, for retrieving that data, and for having other programs use the same data? Warranty, maintenance, and training information should be given in detail to avoid misunderstandings. Model and modification numbers of the hardware components should be included.

The software programs to be used should be listed by title and release identification. Describe the responsibilities and ramifications that will result if these programs are locally modified. Furthermore, the basic software packages will be upgraded in time, and Golden Byte and Vineyard Pipe both should make provisions. The one thing that should not happen is for Vineyard Pipe to find itself up a software creek without a programmer.

If computer system suppliers and their customers can plan and work together, both might survive well into the twenty-first century, and both will certainly be the better for the experience.

CHAPTER 10

The Odd Ones

"Man is the only animal that blushes—or needs to."
- Mark Twain

IT IS ODD, BUT OFTEN TRUE, that the response of the same person to the same stimulus at different times is different. People tend to be unpredictable, but many theorists place managers into well-defined groups based on dominant personalities or on the tendency to use aggressive techniques. For the last forty years or so, managers and behavioral consultants have often offered conflicting rules for improving our skills and attitudes based on these *a priori* groupings. People appear too complex for this rather simple-minded segregation. We exhibit a wide range of personalities and emotions in response to stress and environment, defying simplistic classification. Introducing objectivity into this sometimes random and always subjective world seems a worthwhile managerial task.

Our friend and alter ego, Dilbert, describes odd managers and supervisors extant in today's business world rather bitingly. Unfortunately, his horned supervisor has his archetype in real people. Fortunately, few of us are likely to exhibit this man's full range of faults, but it is interesting and instructive to examine the behavior of odd managers and executives who operate on the fringes of reason, occasionally effectively.

Ingrained company cultures may well encourage an odd management style. One of the more annoying of these counterproductive practices is the invasion of employee privacy in the name of security. **A recent survey of 906 employers found more than sixty-four percent conduct some sort of electronic surveillance of their workers. Thirty-five percent use close electronic surveillance, taping employee telephone conversations and the like.** This surveillance has taken increasing advantage of technology, using miniature devices, reading employee e-mail and listening to voice mail messages, and videotaping employee performance. **About 16 percent of the employers surveyed said that they don't inform their employees that they are under routine surveillance.**

Recently, J.C. Penny Co. settled with a former manager who found that store guards had used a zoom lens on a security camera to watch her chest. These same inquisitive and prurient guards spied on other women through peepholes and a vent in a dressing room. **It is extremely important to carefully select and train security people. There are generally few watchers watching the watchers.**

The continual insistence of odd supervisors and managers to hold long and dull staff meetings at rigidly fixed intervals can be easily corrected by the next-level manager. Valuable time should not be wasted. Staff meetings should be held only when needed, not when the boss feels lonely or because it is Tuesday morning at 9:00 am. These boring meetings typically continue for the full scheduled time and beyond, whether or not there is any useful information passed. Managers scheduling such meetings seem to believe that they are taking the place of timely face-to-face contacts. They do not.

Unreasonable management insistence on particular employee dress and grooming codes with no apparent justification other than the bosses like to see employees looking natty is often cited as a source of employee dissatisfaction. When the employee is in continual contact with the public, there is reason for a dress code. When the employee is working in the bowels of a company facility with no reasonable possibility of contacting customers, safety, comfort, and modesty should be the driving forces behind any rules of dress.

Not too long ago, IBM professional employees typically wore dark suits, white shirts, and somber ties. They were easily recognizable whenever they visited customer facilities. This informal but real dress code extended to the repair and maintenance people, even though the suits and ties often got in the way of their work. Hanging ties can be dangerous when working on moving equipment as they were universally doing. During several years of contact with IBM customer service people, I never saw one even loosen a tie, no matter the heat or proximity to clattering machinery. A few briefly tucked their ties into their shirts to save their lives, but as soon as they felt reasonably safe, the tie was once again hanging according to IBM standard.

In recent surveys, 25% of a cross-section of workers strongly indicated that a prime source of job dissatisfaction is the behavior of the boss. It appears that this dissatisfaction can be directly charged to the behavior of a relatively few odd managers who probably don't know their actions are considered strange. Few people will tell them, and if told, they probably won't listen.

In larger companies, many of these persistent supervisory problems stem from a management style that was developed earlier in the life cycle of the company, and honed over the years. When this style became the norm and formed an integral part of the management culture, these problems became more and more difficult to correct with the passing of time. Propagators train others by example and are themselves further trained by other odd managers who don't recognize the mischief they and their subordinates are causing. Some senior managers make it a practice to use casual personal contact to periodically examine the interaction of employees and their supervisors in order to find and stop any obviously odd practices. This of course doesn't work if the big boss gets out only once every few months.

Some tendencies exhibited by managers may not be odd enough to be considered truly odd, just passing strange. For example, a manager I knew carefully measured the available area in his new office, and compared it to offices of managers of similar rank, complaining bitterly to his new boss that he had ten fewer square inches of office space than some of his colleagues. This individual, who had arrived at his position courtesy of the Peter Principle, left it courtesy of his new boss.

Arrogant odd managers without talent can be particularly disruptive. One very senior man (not the brightest soul) once told me, "I look down on all of you so-called professional people. I expect little loyalty from you, and you should not expect any from me." It's bad enough to think these thoughts, but it is even worse to utter such thoughts. This man had one redeeming quality—he didn't play favorites. He treated everyone equally shamefully. After being subjected to this manager's philosophy, several key engineers left the company. The manager became the president of a U.S. subsidiary of a fairly large European electronics manufacturing firm, but since he took his odd views with him, he didn't last long.

Managers should be intelligent and have a calm demeanor. The next three tales are dedicated to those managers who do not possess these qualities.

The Shrimp Boats Are A-Comin'

In the 1950s, the U.S. deployed a series of small radar-guided, anti-aicraft missile systems called Nikes. Batteries of Nikes were placed near cities thought to be prime targets of Soviet air power.

The eccentric character in this story is a technically oriented professional manager at large West Coast aluminum works. He had been with them for years, probably since he graduated from college, and he held the technical position of chief metallurgist.

Now, the Nike structural design must have been fairly challenging. There were a number of interesting forces acting on the missile. To contain these forces, the designers came up with a shape to support the stubby wings that looked for all the world like a rowboat. A big musical hit at the

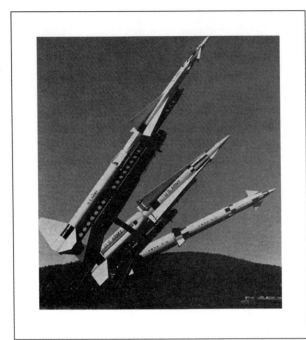

International Encyclopedia of Aviation. 1977. New York: Crown Publishers.

Various Nike Versions on Display

time was Peggy Lee's, *The Shrimp Boats Are A-Comin'*. In honor of this popular tune, the workers at the aluminum supplier who were making parts for the Nikes, dubbed the boat-like part a shrimp boat. These shrimp boats were initially made as aluminum forgings. Forging produces the best aluminum parts, but forging is expensive. Casting is the most common alternate fabrication method. If an alternate method will work, it is generally selected over forging to save money. The military was pressing for lower costs, so during a production discussion with the military customer, the use of alternate shrimp boat fabrication techniques came up.

One of the metallurgists suggested the possibility of plaster mold casting. The chief metallurgist's eyes glowed. He knew real money might be saved by producing the shrimp boat by casting rather than forging. This aluminum supplier had an excellent and temporarily underworked plaster mold shop capable of producing cast parts to almost forging tolerances. Unfortunately, even castings made from precise, selectively chilled plaster molds typically exhibit poorer mechanical properties than forgings. Using the usual casting alloys would not be acceptable. A super high-strength alloy was needed to meet the shrimp boat strength requirements.

There was a little-used casting alloy waiting in the wings. Dubbed 220, this alloy, at first glance, seemed to have a good chance of working. About 10% of the principal alloying constituent of 220 was magnesium. This high magnesium content had been a source of worry to some metallurgists, so the 220 alloy had been little used.

The chief metallurgist knew that all would be well. Patterns and molds were made, sample parts were produced, and to the delight of our chief metallurgist, the strength tests on coupons from the sample shrimp boat castings passed with flying colors. The results were given to the customer, and after a series of discussions, a contract was awarded and the shrimp boats were cast.

The chief metallurgist was a man who took personal credit for any success in his organization regardless of the originator. As soon as the ink was dry on the shrimp boat contract, he had his people write articles about the shrimp boat production for publication in metallurgical and metal fabrication journals. These articles extolled the savings that were accruing from this inventive change. He examined and edited each article, adding a few comments about his own management ability and insight.

This chief metallurgist had a bad habit of constantly and publicly insulting his direct reports. As part of his management style, he demanded that each employee in his department meet with him once a month to justify why that employee should be kept on the payroll. This made for hostile and rather strained relationships. No one in the department would go out of the way to save the chief metallurgist from embarrassment.

When he made a mistake, he was loath to admit it. Once he had hired a meteorologist, thinking the man was a metallurgist. Once he realized his error, he quietly put the meteorologist into a quality control position to take him out of the limelight, hoping that the whole thing would blow over. Once the word was out, this odd personnel error caused a lot of snickering when the chief metallurgist wasn't around.

Time passed. The initial shrimp boat order was quite large, and production was going well. Some of the shrimp boats were stored in a warehouse in Santa Monica. Santa Monica is directly on the shore of the Pacific Ocean and is blessed with cool and salty sea air. Moist salt air tends to become salt water as the temperature cools. If there is a cool surface for this moist air to condense on, it will. In this case, the shrimp boats were cold and available. When magnesium and aluminum are both in contact with salt water, electrolytic corrosion occurs. Meanwhile, magnesium was coming out of the solid solution at the alloy grain boundaries. As a result, micro (and not so micro) internal corrosion of the shrimp boats was proceeding nicely. Chemistry was in action!

Prior to the assembly of the next group of Nikes, sample shrimp boat parts were taken from the damp warehouse and tested. The results were horrid. Ductility is the ability of a material under stress to change its form without breaking. Ductility is a good and necessary quality of structural parts. The shrimp boats weren't ductile anymore. They had corroded and turned brittle. The military inspector notified the aluminum company. Believing the bad test results were due to incompetence, the chief metallurgist ordered new tests. Surprise! The second set of results duplicated the first. Things were not going well, but he had another card to play. He called in his captive meteorologist, now a full-blown statistical quality control engineer by default. The chief metallurgist considered his meteorologist as expendable, and directed him to explain away the bad results using the magic of statistics. In short, he was to make a silk purse out of a shrimp boat.

The poor fellow made a careful examination of the test data and concluded that by any rational standards the shrimp boats were bad. He reported this to the chief metallurgist who told him to find a way to get those parts accepted. His job depended on it. The meteorologist wrote a brief report supporting the earlier position that the shrimp boats should be scrapped. Then he quit. **No one on the metallurgical staff was interested in saving the reputation of a man who commanded so little respect.** Despite a delaying tactic by the chief metallurgist, the remaining parts were rejected and scrapped. The chief metallurgist ate crow. The company had no choice but to replace the rejected shrimp boats with forgings at their expense. The metallurgical magazines were not officially notified of the fiasco, but they found out.

A few things can be gleaned from this story.

Mutual respect between a manager and subordinates is essential. If the chief metallurgist had respected and trusted his people, he would have drawn on their knowledge and experience. The potential for disaster was well known to some of them. Had they been on his side, he would likely have been saved embarrassment by being made aware of the potential flaws in the alloy.

When faced with unpleasant facts, it is best to accept them for what they are. Ignoring or disbelieving them is not likely to make them go away. **When ugly rumors become ugly facts, good managers usually have options for corrective action.** They examine their options carefully and choose the best available one, acting rapidly to minimize the loss.

It is worth reiterating over again that **when dealing with new ideas and new things, it is invariably easier to make the world worse than to make it better.**

Poor Relations

An arrogant and odd chairman of the board of a large, diversified, and publicly traded Fortune 500 company had, by hook and by crook, taken control of the company from its prior management. As soon as he was firmly in command, he saw to it that this company was managed as if it were a closely held family corporation, with the family behaving as though they were laws unto themselves. Company profits of the time were largely dependent on sales to the U.S. Government. Production of aircraft and sophisticated electrical and electromechanical gear to the military services was particularly profitable. Even so, this board chairman cared little for government regulations and procurement policies. He was the antithesis of "Dutch" Kindleberger of North American Aviation who advised his management, "When doing business with the U.S. Government always turn square corners." This applies to all dealings business or otherwise, as well.

Bently IV, the board chairman's son, had just finished college with a physics degree without distinction. Both he and Dad wanted him to rapidly learn the in's and out's of their new and complex business, so the managers of a division working with sophisticated technology were ordered to take Bently under their wing. These people were charged to teach him everything they knew. This was a tall order. Bently was a little dense and very vain. Before, when things didn't go his way, he would call Dad to complain, but now that he was hard at work on his first real job, Mom was often closer. He complained a lot to Mom about unsatisfactory treatment at the hands of the hired help when she picked him up at the close of each day in her chauffeured limousine. She made sure that both Dad and the local management stayed well informed about the manner in which her son was treated.

It was decided that Bently should move from organization to organization about every two months. When it came time for Bently to go to his next broadening experience, eligible managers fought to see who wouldn't get him. The division president decided after the third or fourth of Bently's moves that offering more management sacrifices could be avoided by assigning Bently to his office. The president put Bently under the wing of a Mr. Twiggy, a recently hired consultant assigned to the president's burgeoning staff. Mr. Twiggy was considered by most of the managers to be easily expendable, so most folks were delighted with this turn of events.

Mr. Twiggy had delusions of grandeur. He accepted the assignment to tutor Bently with gusto, hoping to parlay this relationship into an influential position at the corporate level. He knew that he was too valuable a man to stay where he was, particularly when most of the people he had met didn't appreciate him.

Bently and Twiggy each day embarked on tours of the company, freely investigating trouble spots wherever they found them. As Bently and Mr. Twiggy invaded each organization in turn, the alerted management received them by asking them to look into things that might need fixing but would not result in solutions that would hurt too much. This accommodation had been working well when Mr. Twiggy happened to overhear a pair of gyroscope engineers discussing what sounded like a rather serious problem. He understood none of the details, but it seemed to him that Bently's skills could be applied to whatever the problem was.

Before proceeding to the solution, Twiggy and Bently felt they should know a little something about the problem. They met with the director of operations, who knew as little about gyros as they did. The director, being a man of political bent, was happy to help. He called in a product engineer to identify and define the problem. After some discussion, it appeared that the gyro difficulty that Bently and Mr. Twiggy wanted to solve was one of poor yield from a factory station that set and tested motor bias for a large precise marine gyroscope. Mr. Twiggy felt that this was definitely something that he and Bently could easily deal with, and thereby cover themselves with glory. He was already mentally composing his response to the congratulations of the big boss, deprecating his own efforts in favor of kudos to Bently, but in such a way as to let Dad know who was really the brains behind the solution.

Mr. Twiggy's view of gyroscope motor bias was that it had something to do with how accurately the motor was installed. Bias meant slant, so the motors somehow must be incorrectly assembled on a slant. A few measurements and the design of a simple tool were certainly all that would be required to take care of matters. He might even find an acquaintance to write a paper on the subject that he would co-author. (Motor bias refers not to assembly of the motor on the slant, but to the effect of the motor on gyro performance, in particular, gyro precession, or drift). The gyro in question was one of ultra-high performance. Hours of test and retest were required to separate the effects of the motor on gyro precession from other arcane error producing sources. The motor bias problem had been beaten down over several years by the best gyro engineers in the world with reasonable success, but every so often the problem resurfaced and had to be taken care of once more.

After receiving the approval of the operations director to correct the yield at the motor bias test station, Bently and Twiggy headed to the gyro assembly area to view first-hand the problem whose solution had eluded the incompetent gyro engineers. One minor point everyone had missed to date was that the design, manufacture, and performance of this particular gyro was classified "Secret" by the Department of Defense. The assembly was done in a closed clean area, with access allowed only to those having both a secret clearance and a "need to know." The company was bound by contract and by law to obey the rules. Neither Mr. Twiggy nor Bently had ever thought to apply for any kind of a security clearance, so naturally they had none.

When the pair showed up and wanted in, they were politely rebuffed by one of the technicians. Mr. Twiggy pointed out through his teeth that the operations director had given them leave to enter, and, "Oh, by the way, this is Bently, the son of the board chairman." The technician decided that the problem was too big for him, so he called for the assembly area supervisor. Mr. Twiggy demanded entrance from the supervisor, and again received the same response. "No clearance, no need to know, no entry." Mr. Twiggy was so annoyed, he called the operations director, telling him how his words had meant nothing to his underlings. The director imme-diately called Jim, the manufacturing manager who was responsible for the gyro factory. The director ordered, "Let Bently and Twiggy into that clean area, clearance or no clearance." The director hung up without allowing Jim to reply and went on a long lunch break.

This put Jim in a difficult, if not impossible, position. Jim was an honest, capable, and conscientious manager. He knew that Bently and Mr. Twiggy had no business in the secret area, but he had a clear and direct order from his boss to let them in. When the pair came back to the entry door, Jim was there. After as much thought as he had time for, he decided to deny them admittance despite the order from the operations director. When Jim told Bently it was impossible for him to be permitted to enter without a proper security clearance, Bently was livid. Spurred on by Mr. Twiggy, Bently threatened Jim with instant dismissal. Jim stood fast, so Bently called Dad.

Dad was on the East coast, it took some time to get him to the telephone. Bently felt ignored, and he didn't like to be ignored. When Dad finally came on the line, Bently embellished the story. He told Dad he was being kept out of the gyro factory because the managers didn't want their incompetence exposed. In particular, there was a pipsqueak factory manager named Jim who had given them some lame excuse having to do with military security that Bently was sure had been trumped up. Dad went ballistic, saying. "It is my factory. No one can keep my son out of there!" Dad never dealt directly with working underlings. He had no interest in talking to Jim, rather he had his secretary call the division president. This move had an added advantage in that Dad could give firm orders to a subordinate who was about as familiar with the problem as he was, reducing the likelihood of any objections from that quarter.

The division president wasn't in. George, the operations director who had just come back from lunch, was the nearest the secretary could find. After a few seconds on the phone with irate Dad, George realized that either opportunity or disaster was on his doorstep. He had learned early on which side his bread was buttered, so he promised to swing immediately into action to right the heinous wrong being done to Bently by those "idiots in the gyro factory!" Dad's parting shot was, "If I get another call from Bently asking for any more help on this matter, you're fired," or words to that effect. George gulped and said, "Yes, sir. I understand, sir."

Despite other pressing demands, George immediately left his office and trotted down to the gyro factory. Bently, Mr. Twiggy, and Jim met him at the door. Without waiting for any explanation, George ordered Jim to let Bently and his friend into the factory at once, or he would face the consequences. George was pleased. He thought that he sounded very managerial and decisive. Bently looked impressed. Jim, though, just looked sad. He said, "George I can't let these people in. I resign. You do it."

This was not going the way George had hoped. Through the glow of two lunch-time martinis, George remembered that there were nasty penalties for willful violation of security regulations. It would be so much better if he could get Jim to appear to authorize the entry, so he had another go at ordering him. This time his voice was softer and sweeter. He appealed to Jim's reason, to no avail. By now, all Jim wanted to do was to get away. He wasn't buying anything further, and he left.

George felt now that he had little choice but to let Bently and Mr. Twiggy in. Imagining testifying at his criminal hearing, he said, "This is a classified area, and neither of you have proper clearances nor a need to know, so I am going to ask the floor supervisor to go with you to make sure that you don't inadvertently come across any secret material." What George didn't know, or didn't want to know, was that any view of this gyro was secret. The very act of looking at the gyro motor was a violation of security. Nevertheless, Bently and Mr. Twiggy spent some time perusing the gyro, the motor, the gimballing, and the test setup. Fortunately for national security, it all meant nothing to them. A precision marine gyroscope is a very complicated instrument. The motor doesn't look like most motors. Even an experienced mechanical engineer is not likely to learn a lot about motor bias effects from looking at the motor. It was slowly dawning on our inquisitive pair that the problem was considerably more subtle than either of them could possibly understand. Mr. Twiggy observed quietly to the floor supervisor that he had a potential solution in mind, but since everyone had been so uncooperative, the gyro people would just have to solve their own damn problems. Off they went without so much as a farewell, to find the next trouble spot desperately needing their attention.

Jim left the company, and the company lost the services of a fine manager during a critical period of its existence because of the meddling of a powerful man who should have known better. Jim did the best thing he could do for himself, cut and run. George, Bently, Mr. Twiggy, and Dad all can consider themselves fortunate that no one blew the whistle on them.

Campaign Contribution Chicanery

Stories about the next man's misapplication of power could keep the Harvard Business School in case histories well into the next century. The tale is one of unwarranted, self-serving, and probably illegal meddling of a CEO in the private affairs of company managers.

It all happened during the second Nixon presidential campaign. The "Committee to Reelect the President," better known by its apt acronym, CREEP, had been formed to oversee and encourage contributions to the Nixon ticket. Committee membership included, by design, a large number of influential business people. One of the members was our CEO. It was later rumored that he was looking forward to an ambassadorship in return for delivering his quota of "voluntary" contributions to CREEP. After it was all over, the more charitable suggested the anticipation of this political plum had temporarily clouded his judgement. Others suggested that his judgement had always been cloudy. In any event, he laid thinly veiled demands for contributions to CREEP on nearly all of the company managers, regardless of their political bent. Republicans, democrats, liberals, and peace and freedomers were all tapped to contribute to Nixon's political cause. Fortunately for the CEO, the company legal people were able to convince him that written demands for political contributions from his managers would not be proper. Any such demands made on the behalf of a political candidate would not be looked on with favor by the courts who would surely be involved if written evidence ever came to light, so the arm twisting was all verbal. Meanwhile, Dick Nixon's plumbers were planning to raid the democratic party office in Washington at a place called Watergate.

When rumors of the contribution requests/demands came down through the chain of the company command, they were initially ignored as being blather from the lunatic fringe. Shortly after, missionaries from the corporate office stopped by the various divisions to point out that the expected contribution to CREEP would be one-half of one week's pay from every second-level or higher manager. To get the attention of recalcitrant managers, there was an associated threat that went as follows: "Names will be taken. Those who choose not to contribute to CREEP will no longer be considered team players. There is no room in this company for people who are not team-oriented. In a few instances of financial hardship, contributions may be accepted that are less than the guidelines. Those who want to be treated as full-fledged members of the management team will, of course, contribute the amount recommended in the guidelines."

Local senior executives were visited and browbeaten by corporate representatives when not found completely cooperative. These corporate torpedoes made it clear that the CEO expected contributions of guideline amounts from all eligible managers in each and every division. The senior people were to do the arm-twisting. As the CEO said, "It will be more effective that way."

Times were not good. Perhaps twenty percent of the work force at several of the divisions had recently been laid off. People who were middle managers but a month or two ago, were now pumping gas and feeling fortunate to have found a job.

There was little bargaining power available to the local division managers. Their choices seemed quite clear. Contribute to CREEP and convince others to do likewise or prepare to collect on unemployment insurance. The engineering organizations at one of the larger divisions were several thousand strong, even after serious layoffs. Therefore, there were still a lot of engineering managers eligible to contribute to CREEP. Despite of, and probably because of, the increasing pressure to contribute, the back pressure from these working managers increased as well. The most common questions asked of managers in the hallway were "Are you going to pay CREEP? If so, how much?" It was finally decided by most of those eligible that prudence dictated they should cave in to the extent of contributing something. Making the huge guideline contribution though was out of the question.

When the small engineering contribution checks were counted and the CEO notified, he thought long and hard about his veiled threats. If he took action against those who had contributed less than his guidelines, he would have to demote or fire most of the engineering managers at several divisions without real cause. While he probably found this idea attractive, he elected to do nothing for the moment. His vice president of contributions had kept meticulous records of who had paid and how much. The information would be available for later punitive action.

When Watergate surfaced, later became sooner. Richard Nixon's resignation put quite a different light on matters. The contribution records were nicely filed and intact at the corporate offices. That this information still existed was now cause for panic. New investigations looking into presumed transgressions of the Nixon administration were opening daily. Dirty laundry waved over Washington. Who knew where the investigators would be poking next? Even so, the chairman wouldn't agree to the destruction of the contribution records. The vice president of contributions felt rather differently. He was the record keeper and liable for penalties that only God knew. After some thought and consultation with corporate counsel, he arrived at an innovative solution. He would send all potentially incriminating records down to the managers of the various divisions with instructions to keep the records safe and available. That way, if the chairman wanted them, he need only ask. If any investigator came nosing around, the corporate people would be found to be pure as the driven snow. When the records arrived at the divisions, they were promptly shredded. No rational manager considered for a moment retaining the club with which he would later be beaten.

The whole thing blew over, but the very idea of an entire management team being dunned for political contributions to any candidate is repugnant. Respect for the CEO crumbled. This company's top management was fortunate not to have been subject to adverse legal actions, but what about the next time?

Odd isn't always bad. We are individuals, not statistics. We all have our quirks. Our fellow employees, family, and friends learn to recognize these and deal with them. These foibles don't necessarily make us bad, just interesting. Every so often an individual comes along who is so naturally individual as to be exceedingly odd. Where such people use their eccentricities to further their goals, they often can be more effective in certain environments than less colorful types, but they tend to be single-minded and unconstrained.

The Admiral

Hyman Rickover was an odd one, possibly the oddest admiral ever, in the U.S. Navy. He was an advisor to presidents and the father of our nuclear undersea fleet. He cared not a fig for things said about him. His dedication and his eccentricities made him a legend. He was still on active duty when he was in his eighties.

He could strike terror into subordinates. He personally interviewed all officers who applied for the fleet nuclear programs. His interviews were intended to determine how prospective nuclear officers would respond to the unexpected or behave under stress. Even when civilian contractors discussed him, everyone knew who "the admiral" was.

One lieutenant who had applied for a berth on a fleet ballistic missile boat showed up spic and span for his obligatory interview with the admiral. The lieutenant was ushered into the corner office in Crystal City, Virginia where the admiral held court. The admiral's desk was gun metal gray, placed catercornered, facing the entrance. It was covered with fragile career memorabilia. As the lieutenant came to the front of the desk and smartly saluted, the admiral glared at him and said, "Make me mad." An odd request, at best. The lieutenant, not believing his ears, said, "Sir?" The admiral repeated his order, this time louder, "Make me mad!" Successful lieutenants work long and hard at not making admirals mad, so the lieutenant considered his next move very carefully, finally deciding that the admiral meant what he said. He leveled his right arm, hesitated for a moment, and then swept all of the admiral's valuable mementos off the desk, and sent them crashing to the floor. Admiral Rickover watched in horror as his career shattered before his eyes. He rose, spitting mad. He caught himself, realizing that he had effectively ordered the lieutenant to destroy his priceless artifacts. He took a moment to calm his thoughts and said slowly, "You did what I asked. You made me mad. I approve your application. Now help me pick up what's left of my career."

A Calculating Man

It was the early 1970s, and hand-held calculators were hot items in the world consumer marketplace. Companies like Bomar and Texas Instruments were leading calculator producers. Unicalc was the name of a small but fairly important calculator supplier of the time. Unicalc marketed a line of adequate calculators with the aid of imaginative advertising. For a time, these calculators sold well. Retailers attracted by the Unicalc advertisements were continually bidding against each other for the limited available quantities. This lack of product wasn't the fault of Unicalc. Most of the calculator assemblers relied on the few integrated circuit (IC) suppliers of the day.

The IC (known as the "chip") manufacturers had all been surprised when the increased demand for electronic parts far outstripped their joint production capabilities. There was no way that the limited IC production facilities of the time could meet the demand for these new hot products.

To make matters worse, chip production is an extremely complex and capital-intensive activity. Even today, years are required to bring a new IC production facility on line.

As long as a calculator assembler could find chips somewhere, calculator assembly was the business to be in. To be a successful supplier, one needed only to have access to a chip producer, have an engineer available to put together some schematics and assembly drawings, and have an assembly house—usually in the Orient. Doing business in this fashion required very little capital and yielded excellent returns with little risk. When supply caught up to demand, things would be different. But for a time, Unicalc was courted by a bevy of retailers. The retailers perception of Unicalc was that it was a good solid firm, had salable products, and the price was right.

Unicalc wasn't exactly a solid, well-financed firm. Everything Unicalc did was done on a shoestring. It was a one-man operation. It (he) wasn't troubled by personnel, equipment, and facilities expenses. The Unicalc mode of operation would have brought a warm feeling to the just-in-time folks. The president and owner of Unicalc, Mr. Unicalc, found a pair of engineers to design a calculator around selected sets of production ICs. Even with little at stake, Mr. Unicalc was smart enough to have an alternate source up his sleeve. Armed with the drawings (more sketches than drawings), he negotiated open-ended calculator assembly contracts with at least two Japanese electronic assembly houses. Next, he went to his potential IC suppliers, extracting price and delivery commitments and playing one against the other. With these commitments in hand as evidence of product credibility, he negotiated contracts with several retailers, playing them against each other much as he played the IC and assembly companies.

Once he had a sales contract signed, Mr. Unicalc would give the device supplier(s) his requested (but firm) delivery dates for a batch of calculator chips. Both sides knew that the IC supplier probably wouldn't make the agreed upon delivery dates. Now, personal persuasion came into play. Mr. Unicalc was a master at cajolery. A few days before a promised delivery date, he would sweep in and camp at the chip supplier's executive suite. He would spend as many days there as necessary. He had done enough homework to know the people who would do him the most good. He would stop them in the hall, put his fatherly arm about them, and plead for his chips. He was not above weeping and groveling.

Weeping and groveling usually worked. No one likes to see their father cry. When the supplier finally gave up and delivered, Mr. Unicalc would go to his car and bring in a number of suitcases to be filled with calculator chips. Once the precious devices were in the bag, he would usually pay the chip supplier in cash. He hated paying cash, but given his asset base, he was generally given little choice. He went directly from the IC plant to a non-stop flight to Tokyo.

Once in Japan, he immediately turned to one of the contract assembly companies to create calculators from the chips in his carpetbags. The Japanese at the time were pretty loose about supplying credit, but they have since learned. Irrevocable letters of credit, or something similar, are *de rigueur*. He used credit whenever he could get it. He would delay payment as long as he could (future money being less valuable than present money), but he always paid. Once production began, he would reopen price negotiations with the assembler, pleading poor markets and poor retail prices. He was often able to reduce the assembly prices by several yen, and once talked a Japanese manufacturer into throwing in a three-cent calculator case for free.

As new IC production facilities came into being, supply rapidly exceeded demand. The market was soon flooded with calculators and calculator suppliers. The seller's market in calculators was over. Some who thought it would go on forever went belly up, like Bomar. Rockwell and many others went out of the calculator business, showing significant end-of-business losses. Mr. Unicalc simply walked away taking his profits with him, leaving no inventory, no buildings, and no real company.

Mr. Unicalc was a fascinating character, an entrepreneur par excellence. He was successful at what he did, but he was the antithesis of a good manager. Working for him would have been hell. Little was sacred. Little could be counted upon where he was concerned. To him, the difference between truth and falsehood was not a narrow line, but a very wide fuzzy band. He would use anyone he could, any time he could, and he fully expected others to do the same to him if he ever let them. He was neither loyal nor disloyal. The concept of loyalty in any direction was quite foreign to him.

So go the odd ones. Charisma and color can be valuable management assets. Selfishness and arrogance never are.

CHAPTER 11

The Root of Evil

"As a general rule, nobody has money who ought to have it."

– Disraeli

IT IS HARD TO OVERESTIMATE the importance of fair salary planning. Employees expect to receive fair compensation for their efforts. All salary increases are very welcome for a while. Though, in the long run, salary changes tend to demotivate people about as often as they motivate them. It may seem presumptuous to add to the volumes written about salary management, but the following thoughts may help managers during those dark hours when too little money is available to distribute among too many good people.

A trio of headaches plaguing many managers at least once each year are the employee performance appraisal, the employee ranking, and the employee wage or salary review. **Managers should strongly consider developing a set of personal procedural mechanics to help remove unintended biases from the review process.** Some suggestions follow shortly, since talking about fairness without getting down to cases is much like exhorting people to be good without suggesting how not to be bad.

Performance Appraisals

Any employee performance appraisal should result from an honest assessment of the reviewee's absolute (not relative) worth to the organization. It should include any recommendations for employee performance improvement that the manager feels to be mutually worthwhile. Depending on the manager's personality and desires, tempered by direction from higher-level managers, an appraisal can be fairly formal with the results written and signed by the manager, or it can be relatively informal and verbal. Both methods have their places, but virtually all larger companies and government entities require written performance appraisals prepared using a predetermined format. These appraisals are typically used as basic supporting documentation for a myriad of personnel actions including salary reviews. Smaller companies seem to be less formal in their appraisal processes than larger ones and feel less need for written appraisals—probably because managers and employees are in closer and more frequent contact.

The human tendency to avoid saying negative things about employees to their faces gets in the way of appraising employee performance with complete honesty and objectivity. Many managers sugarcoat their words to make them sound less threatening. This is generally known as tact, but there **is a fine line between tact and dishonesty.** To attempt to make the appraisal narrative match the job performance description, the employee's performance rating may be raised a notch or two beyond truth. The inevitable result is that about half of the people are rated as outstanding, exceeding expectations, or something similar. Employee performance should be correlated with employee rankings. Employee rankings should by correlated with employee salaries (not necessarily salary increases, but certainly salaries). **The performance appraisal should be an important input into the ranking process, but if skewed to the high side, it becomes something to be explained rather something to be used.**

When appraisals are biased upward, there is insufficient reason to recommend diverse salary increases when other factors so indicate. Most often, the result of this bias is a leveling of salary increases with the lower-paid and higher performing people losing out.

In my experience, I found many of the managers reporting to me uncomfortable about being critical of the employee's performance in the formal performance appraisal. **The larger problem of managerial bias seems to be evidenced by managers preparing too many rosy appraisals and, hence, doing a disservice to the truly outstanding.**

To overcome this most human of tendencies, managers should rank everyone in the organization before beginning any formal performance appraisal. This helps to put things in proper perspective, except for that small number of managers who feel everyone in their organization is well above the organizational average. **Ranking before appraising provides an important reasonableness check on the manager's view of individual performance.** If an employee ranked near the bottom of the organization is about to be highly appraised, an error flag should go up. There may be a good reason for this odd action, but there should definitely be a reason. (Perhaps the employee in question is a new hire or a recent transferee and is performing well above expectations). Failing to find a reason for the anomaly, the astute manager will think hard about the lack of correlation between the appraisal and the trial ranking. One or the other, or both may change.

Managers' mixed emotions about the relative effectiveness of infrequent, scheduled formal performance appraisals versus the more frequent informal kind are quite justified. Most experienced managers would agree that daily informal contact results in a better understanding between the employee and the manager than infrequent formal reviews. One can, of course, have it both ways, but the manager should always insure that the written and the spoken word agree.

When performance appraisals primarily consist of informal contacts, the manager should be prepared to provide direction and counsel at any time. Employees should be advised privately at the first opportunity when the manager senses something is amiss. As long as things are going tolerably well, nothing need be written except commendations for unusually valuable contributions. The operative words here are "unusually valuable." Too much of a good thing will reduce the perceived importance and the benefits of this praise.

If an employee's performance has altered measurably over time, it is not a good idea to say one thing while ignoring the latest formal appraisal (possibly prepared some time ago) that says something quite different. When problems of sufficient gravity arise to warrant an unscheduled formal discussion, the gist of the conversation should be written and summarized with a copy given to the employee who should be free to enter comments for the record.

I have found that the common legalistic procedure of asking (requiring) the employee to sign an appraisal document is generally a bad move. The employee may feel that he has just signed a confession to be used against him in the future. Which, of course, is exactly what may happen. A signature might benefit the lawyers later, but stands a good chance of getting in the way of the manager-employee relations now. Whether or not the employee signs should be left entirely to the employee. Certainly no stigma should be attached to the appraisal by using pithy phrases like, "Employee refused/declined to sign."

It seems that **managers universally dislike to prepare, and worse, to discuss performance appraisals with the appraisees.** A heinous practice to be stamped out is that of the manager asking employees to prepare their own appraisals, with the rationalization that the results will be instructive to both manager and employee.

I once had a boss who after several major delays in my scheduled appraisal asked me to do my own. I told him at the time that if I appraised myself, I was going to rate myself outstanding with no obvious faults. If I had known of any faults, I would have corrected them. My boss seemed embarrassed, but after some soul searching, he still decided that my preparing a self-appraisal would be the lesser of the available evils. I appraised myself. My outstanding rating stood up. It was probably undeserved. It became part of my job history. I learned nothing about my manager's perception of my performance. I did nothing to correct any flaws that he may have perceived.

When a manager feels using formal performance appraisals is beneficial (or senior management insists upon it), there are a few considerations that may make the process less onerous for both managers and employee.

Often managers are reluctant to suggest specific plans for correcting identified employee problems. It is so much easier to tell employees they have no discernable faults. Everyone has faults. When the faults are minor and don't adversely affect job performance, there is no need to dwell on them, but when an employee's job performance can be improved, the manager and the employee should talk. In any event, **the manager always owes it to the employees to level with them in a timely fashion.**

Establishing an incorrect history base for the employee by providing unwarranted glowing written performance appraisals is a ticking time bomb. Months, even years, later the appraisal may be found and read by another manager. If not, it is a safe bet that the employee has his or her copy safely stored at home. When the employee's performance wasn't satisfactory in the first place, has deteriorated over time, or both, it is difficult for the most recent manager to get the human resources department to take the necessary corrective action. When the old performance reviews show that the employee has been outstanding, but nothing of the kind has been the case, the manager who is trying to do the right thing is now suspect. Even worse, the employee may not have received the supervisor's real view of his or her performance. This means that the employee has never had a chance to answer criticism or had any reason to change.

When corrective action is indicated, the manager should present no more than two improvement actions to the employee. Generally, little is gained from trying to lay several stiff and difficult requirements for performance improvement on an employee all at once, even if both the employee and the manager agree. The ability to focus on important issues is diffused when too many actions are scheduled for correction.

Rankings

Not only fairness, but also the employee's perception of managerial fairness is an important element in the employee-manager relationship. Many employees watch for indications that the manager prefers or dislikes a particular person or class of people. For an employee ranking to be useful, it must be credible. The manager preparing the ranking must be perceived as being fair and rational. Credibility is particularly important in those organizations where rankings are discussed with employees as a matter of course. Even when management tries to keep the ranking results under wraps, some information (usually quite accurate) often slips out.

Besides the usual care taken to avoid the appearance of bias, there are a couple of things not normally considered that may give rise to accusations of favoritism. When rankings, salary plans, and the like are being prepared, the manager should advise the secretarial staff to be as circumspect as possible. The manager should also minimize closed door meetings with individual employees. Such meetings are often interpreted as giving preferential treatment during these rather sensitive times.

Some managerial preferences are understandable. It is virtually impossible not to hold people who perform assignments well in high esteem. When the time comes to recommend salary increases for a group, however, these increases should result from a carefully considered review process made as objective as possible. The responsible manager should be well above suspicion. **A well-prepared group ranking is a most effective way to introduce objectivity into an otherwise subjective process.**

The difficulty involved in creating a fair and useful ranking of employees working on diverse assignments cannot be underestimated. In an organization of any size, the manager is faced with evaluating the worth to the company of people having varying experience, education, ability, personalities, assignments, and accomplishments. A well-considered ranking provides a useful and unique input to the salary plan and helps immeasurably to remove biases along the way.

Perceived Worth Rankings

A ranking of employees, grouped by classification, is usually the first thing a salary administrator wants from managers. The classification part needs scrutiny. There may be problems undermining the salary plan resulting from segregating the rankings by employee classifications. In organizations using these semi-rigid classification structures, there are so many varied pieces that often only a few employees can be found within each classification. It is common for there to be only one employee in each job class. Ranking by classification for these employees yields no information about their relative worth to the organization.

Salary administrators tend to subdivide work assignments of professionals into a series of groups called maturation classes or something equally uninformative. A set of preset salary ranges usually forms the basis for these groups; for example, technical professionals are in the MTS group (Members of the Technical Staff), scientists are in the S group, and professionals are in the P group. Within classes in these groups, there are usually numerical identifiers ranging from entry level (usually grade I or government service grades GS-3/5) to ready-to-retire grades VII or VIII and GS-16/17+. Salary ranges in these groups typically have a fairly generous overlap. For example, a senior MTS II can legitimately command a higher salary than a less senior MTS III.

Usually, personnel rankings group only, for example, MTS II's only with MTS II's, MTS III's only with III's, and so on. A lot of useful information is lost with this segmentation. If the organization is fortunate enough to have hired a group of crackerjack younger employees, these rankings do not show their worth relative to that of the more experienced employees. It is not correct to presume that because II's are less experienced than V's, the II's are uniformly not as good as the V's. The inherent unfairness of this kind of segmentation is by no means unique to technical professionals. This same presumption is applied to all professional disciplines.

A better course for managers of up to 100 employees is to prepare or supervise the preparation of the ranking of all salaried non-supervisory employees as one group, regardless of their classification. This "perceived worth ranking" should yield maximum information. Such rankings are not common practice, probably because of the initial difficulty of assessing the relative value of dissimilar people working on dissimilar assignments. It is strongly suggested that this comprehensive ranking be prepared with the full participation of all reporting managers. If such a ranking has not been tried before, the results promise to be an eye opener. Among other good things, a lot of frank discussion about people and activities in the organization normally accompany this ranking process. The give and take of managerial discussions about the performance of all employees usually uncovers and discourages unjustified biases and favoritism.

The human resources department and first-line managers alike find ranking people in this manner distasteful. The standard argument against it is as follows: "It is irrational to rank VII's (or equivalents) along with I's and II's. Worse yet, a chemist or a physicist might sneak into the ranking of a group of engineers. Professional employees of different disciplines and different levels of experience are completely different!" These employees are *not* different. They are all trained to think for themselves; they just think along different lines. They may work on different problems and they may or may not advise others, but **they all should be ranked on quality and quantity of their output,** which are both readily observable. There is no downside associated with ranking all of these people together, save that there is more management time involved and more thought required than when putting together the standard segmented ranking set. However, this is time well spent. If, by chance, all the different II's and III's are truly doing work of lower quality or lesser importance than all of the V's, this will be shown no matter what system is used to rank employees. **Excellent employees with less experience or salary who are doing the same work as those employees with higher classifications or higher pay should be ranked together.**

Another assertion for supporting employee ranking by subgroups is that groups and salary structures should parallel those within the industry as a whole. This notion is justified by the availability of salary data generally subdivided by skill sets and derived from data supplied by various companies. Since the companies involved have a vested interest in keeping salaries low, one might ask if the well-known WEMA curves err on the low side. The data generated seems to be presented fairly, although sometimes it is of questionable accuracy and is often segregated oddly.

Many salary administrators rely only on graphs that depict salaries of selected groups of people versus experience levels. The human resource department will argue that if internal job classes are not segregated into the same or equivalent sets, it is impossible to compare internal salaries with those paid outside, making it difficult to determine the competitiveness of the company's salary structure. It is certainly easier to compare salaries among identical job groups. However, it is unusual to find different companies using employee skills in identical ways, not to mention the diverse salaries paid in regional labor markets. Salary comparisons can be had rather easily for larger segments of people, say all computer engineers or all first-line managers. These comparisons are equally valid and should be more informative than those made for smaller groups.

Another argument supporting rigidly controlled job classifications is that it is vital to contain salaries within groups so that managers are prevented from increasing their employees' salaries forever. While this may be a valid concern in some quarters, penalizing employees is not right. Salary curves are useful but only as interesting guides. **The existence of salary curves should not be a justification for constraining the style and usefulness of employee rankings.**

Salaries can be reviewed intelligently only after a measure of the relative worth of each employee to the group as a whole is obtained. The perceived worth ranking, from the most worthy to the least worthy provides such a measure. Superimposing salary information in the form of a simple line extending to the right of the individual's name, as shown in the table below, permits managers to easily determine salary "instickers" and "outstickers." By creating a table like the one below, ranking information is readily available when assessing proposed salary increases. It is common to show the proposed increase as a dotted line extending the present salary. A segmented ranking does not provide the same kind of insight gained by this more comprehensive ranking.

GROUP RANKING

Rank	Name	Monthly Salary $3,000 $4,000 $5,000 $6,000	Years of Exp.	Classification
1	Brown, G	— — — _____|---|	10	S V
2	Pape, H	— — — _____|--|	14	MTS VI
3	Clint, H	— — — _____| -- |	9	P IV
⋮				⋮
17	McLean, K	— — _____|—|	5	S III
⋮				⋮
26	Grange, S	— — — ____|--|	3	MTS II
⋮				⋮
35	Brian, S	— _____|--|	6	S III
36	Smith, K	—_____|	10	MTS IV

A few managers have commented that there is not enough objective information available to do a credible ranking job in this fashion. It isn't easy and mistakes will probably be made, but nothing ventured is nothing gained. The degree of difficulty depends on the experience and willingness of the managers who have to do the rankings. The ranking of diverse disciplines may well be accompanied by mumbling and grumbling from the managers involved. The more diverse the organization, the louder the grumblings. An engineering unit made up of electrical engineers, computer engineers, and mechanical engineers is relatively easy to rank together despite the existence of three different, but allied, disciplines. A product department of ninety people made up of quality control specialists, engineers, sales staff, marketers, financial staff, and logistics specialists presents a more challenging problem.

At this point, observe that there are as many similarities as differences among employees in the most diverse of groups. The ranking process works best where each manager considers these similarities and uses them to structure the ranking. A lawyer in the contracts department should receive different assignments than an MBA employed there. In many cases, they both work on pieces of the same problem. When their efforts are examined critically, the perceptive manager can identify who took a lead role, who was late, and who contributed more to the successes or to the failures. Once common ground has been established, the manager can review each output for both quality and quantity. At this point, there can be a rational ranking relationship.

Where little common ground seems to exist, it is useful to have the reporting managers rank their employees the old way. That is, initially rank employees by discipline or by classification, in preparation for the later full-group ranking. Armed with the segmented rankings, managers can then merge the employees' rankings in open sessions.

Prior to beginning the open ranking sessions, the wise senior manager will issue a ground rule that **all managers should see employee rankings in each group as it was established by each reporting manager. The rankings from all of the groups will then be merged starting with the highest**

ranked person in each group. Where some of the input rankings are segmented, the responsible manager should be asked to pick only the individual he or she feels to be the most valuable to the organization each round. In general, managers know or know about the employees who report to other managers. They always have opinions (possibly biased) regarding the relative worth of these employees. If managers do not know employees outside of their own groups, the company may have bigger problems than forming salary rankings.

One of my personal experiences with ranking occurred when I took over a design engineering organization in which the managers did not have prior experience with this method of ranking. One manager ranked a couple of the employees in his organization far higher than seemed warranted. During the first merger of rankings, there was clear agreement among all the other managers that these highly ranked people should be ranked near the bottom of the department ranking list. This meant all the people in this manager's organization would end up clustered at the bottom of the ranking, driven down by the two employees he had ranked at the top of his list. This of course wasn't fair, so we allowed him some time to reconsider. He and his fellow managers talked it over. He then decided to make changes that eventually were proven to be in the direction of truth. Everyone but the employees who had initially been ranked too high won.

After ranking is completed, the accompanying performance appraisal information should be examined in light of the ranking results. Even when management has tried to correlate ranking with appraisals, there are likely to be problems. A few employees rated outstanding may show up near the bottom of the list, while some rated as marginal might be near the top. The manager should expect a few of these anomalies. There should be a definite set of criteria used to question appraisal/ranking combinations. Some anomalies may be understandable. Others will demand change. A suggested rule is to scrutinize employees who have been ranked and appraised in either of the two top rating grades and then ranked in open session in the bottom 25%. Likewise, scrutinize employees who have been ranked and appraised in either of the two lowest grades and ranked in the open session in the top 25%.

Salary Estimating

In many large organizations the last phase of the official salary planning cycle is initiated by the company salary administrator. The salary administrator usually establishes and monitors the company's salary policies. **Salary policies, like other policies are intended as substitutes for original thought.** It is hoped that all of these policies will be treated as guides and not as rules by managers.

When the administrator and manager meet, the administrator should inform the manager of the funds available for merit and promotional salary increases. In many cases, both salary administrators and senior managers hold back funds from the reporting managers. This practice does not seem to make much sense. Unfortunately, the effect of holding back available funds, even if distributed later, is to level the salary increases. Almost every employee gets some raise. As the available pool of funds shrinks, the most likely place to find funds to pay for minimum increases is from those employees who were going to get the larger increases. This is yet one more act against the interests of the best employees and against those who are relatively underpaid.

After the merit increase pool is defined and the performance appraisals and organizational rankings completed, the magnitude of each salary increase can be considered. I have used this rule to dictate salary increases: **Where lower ranked people are underpaid relative to others in the ranking group, recommend a higher increase for those lower ranked employees to adjust their salaries. Where lower ranked people are overpaid relative to others in the ranking group, recommend a smaller increase for them than for those ranked above who are making less money. Do not consider a larger increase for lower ranked people than for higher ranked people having lower salaries.**

This rule is based on the expectation that management will correct present salary inequities in the future. Although this may never happen, it is a worthy goal. In the organizations I directed, three years was about the earliest employees could be brought to salary parity. The staff was never static long enough to finish the three-year program. We just kept partially correcting salary problems as they arose. New people were continually hired at the market price, often with higher salaries than the employees who had equivalent backgrounds who had been with the organization for a while. Others changed their work habits and their skill level over time (some for the better, some for the worse). The rankings changed. **Salary equality was always a moving target, but always a target nevertheless.**

Experienced employees are usually paid more than inexperienced employees for the same accomplishments. This isn't necessarily bad, but many managers have a great deal of trouble living with this dichotomy. **Experienced people should be able to move easily among a variety of jobs. When we pay more for experience, we are paying for flexibility and a broad knowledge base.** To make these higher salaries worthwhile, managers should use the experienced employees in a variety of assignments and as advisors to the newly hired.

On occasion, senior managers may feel that the professional staff deserves a general increase. This idea is often in vogue when union negotiations are completed and the bargaining unit employees get a uniform raise, or when inflation or penury struck earlier and the present merit increase budget is woefully insufficient. At such junctures, professional unions often come to life and begin organizing. A favored management weapon is the one-time general increase. In almost every case, fair and proper salary management would have made this sort of machination unnecessary. **General increases are most often an admission of management's failure to pay employees properly.**

A major demotivator tied to salary planning results from people knowing (or thinking they know) the salaries or salary increases of their colleagues. In some organizations, the salaries of everyone are routinely published for all to see. Since 90% of the employees perceive themselves to be in the top 10%, they are understandably miffed when they hear about others' salaries. When confronted by an irate individual feeling woefully underpaid relative to another, management often feels justified to observe that the complaining individual simply isn't as good as the other. This might be true, but any such discussion is doomed. **There is no way that a manager could, or should, try to convince anyone that they are less useful or capable than someone else.** It is better to consider the following bit of logic. Given that the employee believes that he or she cannot spend another's salary, a valid and satisfying argument can be made. It goes like this: "Since all people in the group are ranked together and management has a goal of recommending higher salaries for the more valuable people, it follows that a person who is ranked lower and makes a lot of money can only represent a positive good to the higher ranked and lower paid. The natural result of this situation will be for the higher ranked employee to receive higher raises over time until the disparity is eliminated." This argument is not only satisfying, it had better be true.

CHAPTER 12

Expect the Worst

"The best human intelligence is still decidedly barbarous;
it fights in heavy armor and keeps a fool at court."

– Santayana

Competitive Skills Are Mostly Artistic; Only a Few Are Scientific

COMPETING AND NEGOTIATING ARE enjoyable adjuncts of management, particularly when one is successful. The inspiration for this chapter came from the wisdom of several consummate competitors and negotiators with whom I have had the privilege to work. For reasons known best to them, these skilled people never taught or wrote about their experiences and their methods. This is the only time, to my knowledge, that their valuable lessons have been collected, distilled, and presented in print.

The Pollyanna belief that everything will work out for the best doesn't wash in competitive environments. Even the widely held view that the passing of time will make things better, or at least tolerable, doesn't do a lot for those who are continually juggling limited resources to meet imposed schedules. The passing of time without commensurate accomplishment only causes pressures to increase exponentially. Things do not work out for the best without a lot of good planning and hard work, and perhaps not even then.

Competition has been the watchword of the late twentieth century, and it probably will be the theme of the twenty-first. Competition is tough and unforgiving. The old Eastern Bloc is just now finding out how tough and how unforgiving, but we Americans have always known it. Many people are our personal competitors. Friends, colleagues of all descriptions, fellow students, adversaries, and even to a degree our families are competing with us for resources, recognition, and individual satisfaction. Fortunately, we are not involved in a zero sum game. There may be all winners, all losers, or any combination thereof.

Head-to-head negotiations are one of the purest forms of competition and one of the most fun. It is entertaining and educating to watch negotiators in action. Some are very good, and some are awful. As I watched and learned, the good negotiators posted a win every time. The awful ones often didn't even know they had lost. Where there were consummate negotiators on both sides, they always managed to find a satisfactory compromise where both sides won something. They followed a common logic, and there were many similarities in the way they behaved in the negotiating sessions. I observed, formulated, copied, and took the following lessons to heart.

Never lie.

Prepare for the negotiations personally. Learn everything there is to learn about the opposition that time permits; not only about the subject of the negotiation, but about the negotiators, their backgrounds, their strengths, their weaknesses, their families, and friends. To be effective, this preparation should be personally supervised and carefully reviewed. Others on the team may collect information and prepare position statements, but the chief negotiator must thoroughly understand the background and the facts. It is a losing strategy to expect untutored supporting experts are able to provide information sufficient to carry the day. The chief negotiator must always be able to withstand what I call "first-order questions." Answers to these questions require a fundamental, but not a detailed, grasp of cogent material surrounding the negotiations.

Always clearly determine limits of authority before entering negotiations. If higher management says, "We'll decide how to play it later, based on how the negotiation is going," or "Do the best you can," tell them to find another negotiator. You'll continually wonder whether or not you have the right to consummate the agreement on the table. The other side will quickly determine that you don't have authority. What's worse, no matter what happens, you won't win this one in the eyes of your management. What's still worse, with no scale to measure success or failure, your management now has a built-in fall guy.

Never schedule anything to conflict with the negotiating session. If negotiations are important enough to hold, they are important enough to be your first, second, and third priority. This includes your personal time.

Never guess at facts. Speculation or use of alternate scenarios during negotiations is a good tool, but don't try to pass off as a fact something you're not sure of. Never try to snow the opposition with guesses.

Some bluffing is OK. It is not only OK, it is expected. It is never necessary or even desirable to lie when bluffing. There are always possible future scenarios that can be called into play. Never become so enamored of any bluff that you or your side begins to believe it.

Be polite. Always let the opposition speak first. Give them the opportunity to commit the first blunder.

Listen and look very carefully. Pay attention not only to what is said, but how it is said. Get to know and understand the mannerisms of the opposing team.

Never interrupt. This has been the most difficult of rules for me to follow. The more a person talks, the more he or she gives away. If you are well prepared, nothing the opposition says is likely to convince you of the error of your ways. Take advantage of this free offer to evaluate the opposition. **Unlike football, the side with the most time of possession generally loses.**

Speak briefly and clearly. Start off by stating the benefits to them resulting from accepting your position. If anything, say too little, rather than too much.

Have a specific proposal on the table at all times. If the initial proposal is made by the other side and it is not acceptable, counter with a proposal clearly stating the position of the good guys. The subsequent dialog will, at least, scope the immediate problem.

Never even hint at priorities or at a minimum acceptable outcome. A plethora of negotiations have degenerated into a final grudging acceptance of a predetermined fall-back position because of an inadvertent (sometimes advertent) disclosure that found its way to the opposition.

Never get angry or ridicule the opposition. A bit of floorshow at the right time can work very well. However, just because the negotiator acts irritated, he or she shouldn't get caught up in the action and begin to think anyone is really being wronged. Ridicule might work occasionally, but the ridiculee is likely to return the favor. If this person is sharp, the retaliations can easily hamper negotiations. If not, it's probably not productive to launch an attack.

Know when to quit. There are occasions when the opposing factions are so far apart that no amount of negotiation will accomplish anything. Rather than continue to hammer away and harden the respective positions, consider adjourning or terminating the negotiations. If both sides are really interested in a deal, consideration back at home will likely result in a softening of positions. Subsequent negotiations can then take place on a more rational basis.

These above rules can be applied in situations other than negotiating. I have found these rules to be valuable as guides to behavior in the conduct of competitive briefings and in a number of other adversarial situations. I highly recommend them to you. They have served me well.

The Japanese Advocate

Negotiators in the Western world expect that legal representatives will have much to say during negotiations. They will supply the "right" contract words at the drop of a hat, lead the draft document review, question vague words and phrases, and suggest points of agreement. All of this they do, or try to do, without having a deep understanding of the proceedings. They are *ex-officio* (sometimes not so *ex-*) members of the team, and they are always treated with the utmost respect by both sides.

It wasn't too long ago that some integrated circuit licensing negotiations were about to begin in Japan between two semiconductor giants, one American and one Japanese. The Japanese, being sticklers for form, provided a large quiet room for the discussions. The principals were seated facing each other on identical couches, raised above floor level, complete with antimacassars and ebony coffee tables. The support people on both sides made do with sets of chairs placed on the floor, except for the Japanese lawyer. He wasn't part of the initial gathering. Only after the obligatory exchange of business cards was he permitted to join the group. There was no chair for him. He brought in his own low stool. Once he set his stool down, he began to politely pass out his business cards. The other Japanese who were present had colored cards with names and titles imprinted on both sides, one side in Japanese and one side in English. The lawyer had only a set of simple one-sided black and white business cards on which he had laboriously typed his name in English. After passing out his cards, he sat down. He was quite tall, approaching six feet. Once he sat on his stool, he peered at the proceedings through his knees.

It was time to open negotiations. That is to say, polite conversation began with each principal inquiring after each other's health, family, and happiness. After perhaps fifteen minutes of small talk between the principals, aided by an interpreter, the lesser lights were permitted a few minutes of banter. At the unhurried completion of these discussions, negotiations really began. The Japanese principal opened by congratulating his American counterpart for the excellent results shown in the latest annual report of his company. Lest anyone think this was mere politeness, the Japanese negotiator was setting the stage so that he might later obliquely note that the American company had plenty of money and business, and therefore was quite able to pay for whatever they might receive. The exchange of rights to produce and sell a selected set of each other's integrated circuits was the crux of the negotiations. There were ten Japanese and eight American products available for consideration. The issues were what would be exchanged for what and whether or not any money would be thrown in.

The Americans allowed the Japanese to speak first. The Japanese negotiator spent the better part of an hour describing the products available for trade and extolling their virtues, but he didn't seem to know their characteristics in depth. The Americans listened politely. They had done their homework and knew what Japanese parts they wanted, and what their worth was in trade. They also noted that the Japanese spent a disproportionate amount of time discussing three of the parts. It appeared that the Japanese felt that these were the more valuable, that they were anxious to see them traded, or both. Perhaps they needed a second source. The initial American intent was to trade four of their parts for five Japanese, but with this added information they might do a bit better.

When the Japanese concluded the opening remarks without making a definite proposal, the senior American said simply, "We want you to consider the exchange of two of our parts for five of yours." He then named the parts, both Japanese and American. None of the three that had seemed so special to the Japanese were included. After the interpreter translated the opening American offer, a brief trace of annoyance showed on the faces of several of the Japanese. After some discussion, the Japanese offered a counterproposal.

The Japanese offer boiled down to an exchange of three American parts for five Japanese parts. The package included all of the three parts that had been not so subtly "sold" by the Japanese earlier. The Japanese lawyer, responding to cue, brought out a cross-license agreement written in English and handed it to the senior American, who immediately handed it to the team lawyer for review. All the while, the Japanese lawyer said nothing. Japanese advocates tend to be seen and not heard—a rather pleasant touch.

Without looking at the Japanese agreement, the American lawyer handed the Japanese lawyer an American-prepared version of a proposed exchange agreement, written in Japanese. The American lawyer spoke beautifully about the inherent fairness contained therein. The Japanese team paid polite, but little, attention. After saying his piece, the lawyer then left the room to review the Japanese document. The senior Japanese curtly took the agreement from his lawyer, and without a word began to read. Everything stopped while he read. When he finished, he nodded. This was a form of the Japanese "yes." It meant, "I understand," not "I agree."

Discussion continued. Each time the Americans stated their position, the Japanese listened and nodded. The Japanese reiterated the characteristics of the three parts they were touting without responding directly to the Americans. The American lawyer returned. He told the group that the Japanese agreement, with two exceptions, would be acceptable. Eyebrows raised on the Japanese side. Lawyers didn't tell anything to senior people. They had to ask and then only when permitted. When the Japanese lawyer received the draft changes, he bowed slightly and immediately gave them to the leader without speaking or looking at them. Again everything stopped while the senior Japanese negotiator perused the proposed changes.

After a bit, the senior American checked his watch, sighed, and said that he had the authority to add an additional American part to the original offer and substitute one of the parts that the Japanese seemingly wanted to trade. The Japanese negotiators' response was to repeat their first offer and to observe that any agreement must be on the basis of the Japanese-prepared license document, unchanged. The American contingent was prepared for this apparent intransigence. The leader said sadly, "It appears we will not be able to conclude an agreement today." So saying, the Americans picked up and walked out. The Japanese team stoically watched. When the Americans were at the elevator, the Japanese lawyer ran after them. In halting English he asked them to return. So they did. All was quiet as they reseated. Finally, the senior Japanese spoke. He would agree to the licensing changes proposed by the Americans if they would accept the Japanese version of the parts trade.

The agreement changes were relatively unimportant. The Americans immediately made a counterproposal. They would accept the Japanese agreement as it was if the Japanese would agree to the American-style parts exchange. The American lawyer started to say something, but thought better of it, and said nothing. Once again there was silence. The Japanese negotiator finally shook his head. The Americans slowly began their second walk. This time no one came to ask them back. They rode the elevator to the lobby. The senior American told the group to wait while he called for a pair of taxis. He took his time.

The taxis arrived. The Americans were slow to get in, the senior man was the last to enter the second taxi. The Japanese senior negotiator, the interpreter, and the lawyer appeared as if by magic. The American version of the trade was acceptable. The negotiations were concluded by a handshake. Written paper would follow. The senior American breathed a sigh of relief. He was sure they would be called back the first time, but not sure what would happen the second time, so he gave the Japanese plenty of time to consider. The agreement was basically fair. The Japanese received a license for three valuable American parts, and now had a second source they badly needed for one of theirs. The Americans got a bit more than they had to have, but not more than they expected. The American lawyer was miffed that his advice was ignored. The Japanese lawyer went back upstairs to get his stool.

The Missionary Tale

Negotiations need not be conducted across a table. There are many ways for two sides to compete. Not too many years ago, the missile division of a large military contractor found itself fending off an attack by an equally strong competitor. The principal negotiator/briefer for the missile division was the division's chief scientist.

The management of the missile division knew it was about to be embroiled in a difficult and sensitive product discussion and negotiation, with a lot riding on the outcome. The problem had been festering for some time, and it was now coming to a head. Early on, the missile division had managed to snag the design and production contract for a major piece of missile ground support equipment identified as a guidance and control coupler. This snagging had been done under the collective noses of Northwest Aircraft, which had won both the structural and the ground support contracts for the missile. Northwest wanted the coupler program in its fold at the first opportunity. It was an emotional as well as a financial issue with them. They bided their time, sniping along the way, and they decided to take their shot at the upcoming contract change point. To start things rolling, Northwest Aircraft people finished putting the final touches on an unsolicited proposal to the Air Force. Northwest's timing was excellent. The proposal arrived at the Air Force door just as the procurement department was preparing the follow-on contracts.

The proposal argued that Northwest could provide an advanced design, prove that it would work, and produce the new unit for less money than the missile division. This got the attention of the Air Force procurement department. Being suspicious of contractors' economics, they wanted to see all of the facts displayed in an open session with both parties attending. While this wouldn't be a formal negotiation with a third party present, it had all of the elements of careful preparation, adversarial give and take, bluffing, and role-playing.

Because of the time constraints in fielding the next version of the missile, the Air Force would decide the fate of the coupler from carefully monitored information presented at this single meeting. The unstated hope of the Air Force was that the two contractors could arrive at a meeting of minds, while trimming costs from the redesign and production of the coupler. This would save the Air Force from making a decision that was sure to upset at least one associate contractor. The missile division's chief scientist had been instrumental in creating the coupler design criteria early in the program. He had been key to taking the business away from Northwest in the first place, but did not know that Northwest was involved in this recent attack.

As soon as the meeting date and place were set, the chief scientist began his missionary work. He initiated several informal contacts with Air Force management people and representatives from Northwest. These get-togethers were generally held at a quiet restaurant or bar after business hours. The conversation was usually started by someone from the Air Force or from Northwest. The chief scientist would join in occasionally, gently directing the discussion and listening. He would throw in questions and comments to keep things going along lines he believed could be useful. This missionary work often uncovered prior unspoken concerns of the Air Force. Offhand truths emanating from any of the players would usually show up after the second or third drink. Elements of heretofore submerged dissension surfaced as well.

When dealing with a team of adversaries, it helps to recognize that they often aren't really a team, but a collection of individuals possessing their own aspirations and their own faults. Over drinks or coffee, people often give away a lot. A person can learn a great deal from listening to how things are said and noting the things that are not said. I have been in after-hours discussions where both sides have each had heated arguments with their own people in front of the combined group. These exchanges were often very embarrassing, but at the same time, very instructive. The dedicated negotiator won't enter into these emotionally charged discussions or take sides. It is much better just to sit and listen.

Even when people are acting or positioning, they may well be giving something away. Before a member of a negotiating team gets within a country mile of a member of the opposite team, the 'party line' had better be well ingrained to prevent inadvertent slips. A sometimes unpleasant, but important job, is to identify members of the team who have a tendency to talk too much. If their knowledge and value outweighs the danger of their giving away too much information to the competition, they should be kept on the team but away from the opposition, except in formal meetings where they can be controlled. Assigning important and individual assignments to these employees is a good way of keeping them out of harm's way.

The missile division was to be the meeting host. Prior to these all-important discussions, the chief scientist called a joint planning session with the senior people from both the Air Force and Northwest to set the meeting agenda. This gave him an excellent opportunity to direct the agenda discussions to his liking. During this session, he learned that the Air Force expected a complete and very detailed story from Northwest Aircraft. It appeared, too, that the Air Force wanted more detail than Northwest seemed prepared to provide at the moment. In particular, during the question and answer portion of the upcoming meeting, the Air Force expected Northwest to satisfactorily address all cogent questions posed by the missile division team. Northwest was not allowed to respond with "We will take the question under advisement and provide you with an answer in a few days."

During this session, the chief scientist was introduced to a recently hired senior and highly skilled individual from Northwest. Even though he was new to the program, he seemed very well prepared. He looked like a real threat and seemed likely to be tapped to lead the charge for Northwest.

As the evening wore on, and the talk gravitated toward personal things. It surfaced that this fellow was romancing a girl back home in Seattle. He was serious about her, but she had other suitors.

During a late missionary visit to the Air Force offices, the chief scientist heard about a concern stemming from the National Security Agency. They were worried that command and control integrity of the weapons system might, in some way, be compromised by a change of the coupler, so security was to be a major item on the agenda of the fast approaching meeting. Someone from the Air Force made an offhand comment at lunch that there might be some trouble between the Northwest engineer who had been in charge of the proposal up to now and the brilliant upstart who had just replaced him.

Over the next few days, additional information went into the data bank. The chief scientist learned the senior Air Force representative's favorite type of drink. This was mildly interesting, but not particularly useful. However, he did learn that the highly intelligent threat from Northwest, now the team leader, had made a reservation for a flight back home right after the meeting. His airplane was to leave at about 6:00 p.m. to arrive in Seattle around 8:00 p.m.

On meeting day, the contingent from Northwest arrived in force, complete with a vice president to show the flag. Their team had with them a thick stack of briefing charts, indicating that they were now well prepared to make their case in exquisite detail. Promptly at 8:00 a.m., the Air Force representative called the meeting to order and gave the floor to Northwest.

The team leader was brilliant. His briefing was clear and concise. After presenting the information on about fifteen well-prepared charts, it appeared that the Air Force program manager was fast becoming a believer in Northwest's tale. At this point, the chief scientist politely asked, "Will you take questions as they arise?" The Northwest team leader saw no harm in answering questions as they came up. After that the chief scientist asked a question or two every few minutes, generally for "clarification of technical details." The questions were well spaced. They did not come often enough to be annoying to the Air Force, but often enough to significantly delay the briefing. These were all questions the chief scientist knew the answers to, but few others did. This was not like the chief scientist. He was generally very frugal with the use of meeting time. By noon, the presentation had gotten through only about twenty-five of the seventy charts.

After a short lunch break, it was clear to the Northwest people that they had to speed things up if they expected to complete the presentation before the wee hours. The shrewd Northwest leader announced that because they were now running late, they could no longer take questions from the floor, but would answer all questions at the end of the formal presentation. After consulting his watch, the chief heartily concurred, observing that he for one was very interested in completely understanding the Northwest position. As the afternoon presentation wore on, the missile division people made copious notes of bothersome items from which to formulate questions. By break time, they had collectively amassed one hundred questions. At 5:00 p.m., there were still fifteen charts full of information to present when Northwest called a halt to the proceedings. The team leader apologized profusely, saying that there was still some important material yet to present, but it was vital that he make his scheduled flight. His assistant had his full confidence and would now take over. So saying, he dashed away.

The man who stepped to the podium was the old leader who had been recently deposed. It was immediately obvious that he was ill-prepared, and that he and the new leader had little or no communication. It is difficult to talk effectively while reading from a set of charts you don't fully understand. After several embarrassing minutes, the chief scientist offered to help both sides by answering a few questions that had by now occurred to several people in the audience. He then stepped up and using a few of the Northwest charts, he formulated the questions that he was about to answer. The Northwest man was so relieved to be off the hook that he happily stood back and listened.

That was the end of the Northwest briefing. As the chief scientist posed questions, he pointed out how solutions were already mechanized in the missile division coupler. He made reference to possible National Security Agency concerns about Northwest changes to the coupler design. The Air Force project manager picked up and began to ask detailed questions.

The chief scientist fielded them with ease, then turned to the Northwest representative asking for comments. The man hadn't been listening. He hadn't a clue. The curtain rang down by the Air Force project manager observing that the coupler production should remain with missile division, thanking Northwest for their good efforts in the interest of cost savings.

A few people from missile division went for a drink or two before going home. Well into the first martini, one of the senior missile division managers observed that the chief's missionary work had certainly come in handy. Knowing that the prime opponent probably had a date in Seattle that he couldn't break was useful in the extreme. A little forced delay was just what the doctor ordered. Hearing about the security agency's concerns didn't hurt either. The chief scientist sat back, smiled and said, "I didn't plan for any of that, it just happened." Sure it did!

The Case of the Much-Too-Modern Space Vehicle

By the time top management seriously reviewed it, $200 million had been spent on the design of the avionics suite of a major space vehicle. The suite consisted of inertial navigators, computers, accelerometers, various other sensors, error checking modules, displays, and several miles of cabling and shielding.

This design work was done jointly by a team of engineers from NASA and SPACE, a major NASA systems contractor. The lead engineers from both sides were clearly visionaries. There was little called for in the joint avionics design that wasn't state of the art or beyond. When the top NASA officials finally examined the potential dangers to the program created by using unproven hardware, they were deeply concerned.

To make matters worse, SQV, a major SPACE competitor, smelled blood and had examined and then ridiculed the joint design. Sensing a real opportunity, SQV quickly fleshed out an alternate design. It began lobbying NASA at once with the message that SQV was ready, willing, and able to serve as an immediate down-to-earth replacement for the present avionics contractor. SQV politely pointed out that while the vehicle might be a spaceship, the twenty-fifth century was still a long way off. Top managers at NASA listened and tacitly agreed.

The management at SPACE didn't become leaders in space by rolling over for the first upstart to come down the pike. They quickly assessed the danger and swung into high gear. The top man of the corporation, a man high on action and low on sympathy, passed the word that jobs several layers deep at SPACE would be sacrificed if SPACE didn't hang on to the avionics contract. The vehicle program manager, now highly interested, sought instant help from the corporation avionics experts. These engineers had proven several times over that they could design and build hardware that worked most of the time. In fact, their vice president of research was coming off a string of successes, and was available to deal with this issue. He was immediately drafted and given the authority to do whatever he thought necessary to keep the avionics program at SPACE. By so doing, he could save a lot of jobs. It was pointed out that one of the jobs he could save was his own.

With everyone so well motivated, the real work began. The first task was to put together a team of people who had both the reputation and the ability to identify likely problems with the preliminary design and to change it before the competition became too great. The team consisted of five people with diverse technical backgrounds. First was the president of a premier software house that had been successfully involved in other space programs. Next, the VP picked a man who had pioneered submarine navigation programs. The other team members consisted of a man who had developed programming techniques, simulations, and communication methods for ballistic and cruise missiles; a logistic and fault isolation specialist; and a senior electrical engineer with considerable experience in avionics design.

These people knew the vagaries of hardware and software. They had seen the bitter realities the morning after promised new equipment was to have been delivered in perfect working order. The expectation that an entire set of new, highly complex computing and navigation equipment could be made to work for the first time together in a new space vehicle was unlikely to the point of being ludicrous. The team set out to find equipment that was in production and working and that could be seen, felt, and tested. As it turned out, there were plenty of candidates.

All the available systems and subsystems had shortcomings when compared to their counterparts in the original design, but their characteristics were well-known and proven. To integrate and use this gear in a design that would perform substantially to the vehicle specifications, an entirely new set of defining paper would have to be generated. The behavior of the avionics would change somewhat, principally in the areas of fault isolation and computer system redundancy. More hardware would be needed. Computation rates were slower. The navigation system wasn't quite as good as the paper one, but it met the vehicle requirements. On the plus side, test data was available on everything. **Advertised performance for nonexistent hardware and software is always superior to test data on the real thing.**

After a few weeks, the outline of a new conservative avionics system evolved. It was one that cost less and weighed slightly more than the official configuration. Up to that point, no one outside the team knew what was to come out. Furthermore, the existence of the team was not advertised. The thinking was that if the designers who initially created the design didn't know that a group was working to change what they had done, the rebuttal preparation time would be minimized for the team. While this was a little unfair, the exotic design had been carefully crafted over many months of concentrated work by more than 200 people, and it was presented as a finished product.

As the new system took shape, some of the NASA managers privy to the team's progress took this effort as an opportunity to add and modify some requirements. While members of the team suggested the establishment of an ad hoc change control board dedicated to no changes, the VP counseled cooperation. He pointed out that requirement changes would tend to force modifications to the original design without any suggestion of blame falling on the prior designers. This would, in turn, make the job of selling the new design much easier. The argument made good sense, so the team set out to accommodate those proposed changes that appeared reasonable.

Now that the door was slightly ajar, these executives asked for reinstatement of their favorite features that had been dropped along the way during the first study. Guided by the VP, the team tried to insure that at least one good idea from each of these folks was re-included. In response to a strong suggestion from a senior NASA person, the team decided to use two substantially different computers in the triply redundant avionics computer set to guard against any undiscovered functional flaw in a single computer design.

The NASA technical monitor watching the process began to believe that the new design might be valuable and thus real. Meanwhile, by agreement, any presentation to NASA management requested by SQV or any other avionics competitor to SPACE was delayed until the team could make its full report.

The team rapidly completed its system definition. Block diagrams were readied. Timing diagrams were prepared. Software, computers, sensors, and display modules were selected. Fault isolation techniques were examined. The design was reviewed to insure that the proposed system had the capability of meeting all of the included requirements. Briefing charts were prepared. They were handwritten, mostly by the VP who wanted to insure that they contained exactly what he wanted to say. The entire top-level briefing consisted of only twenty-seven charts. Three briefings for NASA personnel were scheduled in rapid order. No advanced information was released. The first briefing was for top-level NASA managers. The VP insisted that this briefing take place in the afternoon in California. Given NASA management concurrence, the second briefing was destined for the next two tiers of NASA managers and was scheduled early the next day in Houston. The audience there was expected to number about thirty. A third set of briefings was scheduled for later in the day in Houston for the rest of the interested managers and staff. The scheduling was no accident. If the top people could be convinced, then the next group had to be reached rapidly with the design presented in a positive light, coupled with the message that their bosses had heard and substantially agreed. It was essential that this be done before that group could get enough detail of what was going on to get together and plan an effective counterattack. Holding the first briefing late in the day in California, made it less likely that the Houston managers could find out enough to prepare any kind of rebuttal for the next day.

The top NASA executives didn't really believe that a team of six could accomplish much in a few weeks. They had authorized the study principally to blunt the objections of SPACE if NASA found it necessary to contract with a new and more down-to-earth supplier. NASA could say with a straight face that SPACE had been given a chance to put things right. Never mind that NASA engineers had a piece of the problem. The NASA executives would politely listen to the team briefing.

The VP was a consummate briefer, and his reputation was impeccable. His information was well prepared. While he wasn't well known to the NASA executives and managers, the SPACE vehicle program manager made sure that the VP's reputation was spread far and wide. After the second or third chart, the NASA executives began to listen, realizing they were hearing a man who knew what he was talking about. He was a very unusual vice president. Now they were interested and began to ask questions. They could find no holes in the proposed system design. The few people from NASA who had successfully provided inputs to the new design criteria, and who were at this meeting, offered support. The system met requirements that the original design failed to meet. Granted a lot more work was needed, but this was to be expected. The original design would have required an overhaul anyway to meet the new requirements.

At the end of the briefing, the top NASA executive asked for a brief caucus with the others from NASA. The SPACE representatives sat through a short but agonizing wait before the NASA contingent reappeared with the announcement that they had decided to accept the team's recommendations. They authorized the team members to proceed to Houston to brief the NASA managers and engineers there. The rest was relatively easy. NASA in California immediately made this statement to NASA in Houston: "Despite a prior lack of confidence, we now believe the team's approach is correct and that its avionics design is sound. Details are fair game, but the fundamental approach is not."

The Houston staff listened attentively to the VP. More questions were forthcoming, but were answered to the satisfaction of most of the NASA engineers. The briefing closed with general concurrence. All but two NASA engineering managers stated they were in agreement. The team members noted the names of these people so that private discussions could be held with them later.

The final briefings were held that afternoon. The SPACE team members asked two or three of the more positive NASA people to introduce the speakers with a few positive comments. By now the VP was talked out. Other members of the team took over. It was amazing how little flack came back since the audience was composed of people who had sweated blood on the original design. The fact that their bosses had just stated that three levels of NASA management had bought into the new conservative system muted most opposition. After satisfactory private discussions with the people who had questions, including the two dissenting managers, the team left for home.

Now that the team design was validated at NASA, an avionics engineering organization was put in place at SPACE to insure everything was nailed down. New detailed specifications had to be prepared with dispatch. Subcontracts had to be let quickly. There was still a formidable competitor chomping at the bit who had been held off for a time, but now would be unleashed, if only to provide food for thought for NASA management. The team stayed together long enough to acquaint the new leaders with everything the team had done and to insure that the new organization was beginning to operate effectively.

The vice president of research orchestrated the success of this particular venture. There was a lot riding on the outcome, so he acted accordingly. Much of his waking time had been spent in insuring the technical adequacy of the design that the team was evolving. Perhaps even more importantly, he devoted a great deal of time and effort to understanding the views and the personalities of the NASA players. **As in most significant engineering decisions, it was vital that the technical and the human elements played in harmony.** The timing of the series of NASA briefings was a master stroke. Had the NASA designers been given time to defend their positions, it is certain they could have done a credible job, almost certainly delaying a final decision. **All designs are compromises to a greater or lesser degree and all are subject to varied criticism.** The avionics waters would have been muddied, and NASA management might not have felt confident enough to render a swift and clear-cut decision. It is possible that the competition would have been asked by NASA to act as referee, critiquing both system designs. This would have given them an excellent opportunity to peddle their wares to the program. That none of this happened is to the credit of the VP and to the team.

Appendix

This appendix provides supporting detail regarding the MAC-TEC restructuring discussed in Chapter 2. Presented below are the methods used to create the three focused businesses from the single diverse MAC-TEC functional organization.

MAC-TEC Electronics was fortunate that a new CEO/general manager with years of experience at MAC-TEC had taken over the reins. He had experienced several management problems resulting from the MAC-TEC functional organization described Chapter 2. He forecasted that the systems businesses would grow rapidly for some time, and he was uncomfortable locking them into what would almost certainly migrate to a complex matrix structure, feeling it was past time to consider simplifying organizational changes. To clarify his thinking, he made out a list of conflicts similar to the one in Chapter 2. He wanted a less combative structure for MAC-TEC. He decided to try a PPorP organization, and he used the following steps.

1. The MAC-TEC CEO first listed the products, projects, programs, or services that were the prime outputs of the company. He formed three separate and distinct businesses that would do the job to his satisfaction. He was careful to define the roles of each with no overlap in the definition.

2. Next, he identified a trial set of functional organizations to be merged or distributed into each of the planned PPorP businesses. In some companies other than MAC-TEC, the design and manufacturing/ product engineering groups might be really different from each other, in others not. For MAC-TEC, they could be easily merged. Similarly, the marketing and sales groups might be different enough to warrant organizational separation in some companies, but not in others. After these and other similar considerations, the MAC-TEC CEO outlined what he considered the best organization. The top level is shown in the figure below. To his mind, this grouping exhibited the fewest potential second-level conflicts.

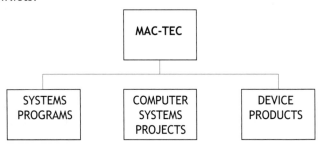

MAC-TEC CEO's Best Organization

3. Next, he examined and listed all central and service functions, and divided these functions into two groups. Group 1 was composed of functions principally engaged in designing or producing products or engaged in serving customers, but whose employees and services were distributed and timeshared among the products, projects, or programs. Some examples of the functions included in Group 1 were as follows:

Research—For companies engaged in pure research, it is best to leave that function intact, but where possible, the applied research function should be moved into the PPorP organization it serves.

Central Computing—where it still exists.

Information Systems.

Drafting—where this function is separate from engineering.

Manufacturing.

Marketing and Sales.

Group 2 was composed of everyone else who did not fall into Group 1, and who performed central functions for MAC-TEC. Some of the functions included in Group 2 were as follows:

Plant Maintenance.
Security.
Personnel (Human Resources).
Legal.

4. Next, the CEO listed the supporting functions he felt should be included in each of the three businesses, as shown in the figure below. He noted the pros and cons and after careful consideration, he thought that a complete restructuring of MAC-TEC into this best organization was too much change to accomplish all at once without adverse effects on the systems businesses.

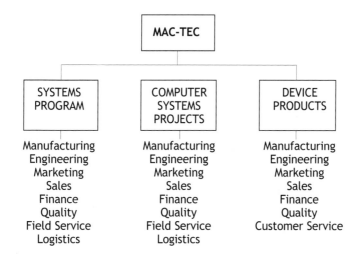

The MAC-TEC Best Organization With Supporting Functions

The CEO felt that it was best to divide the Group 2 functions among each of the businesses.

At this point, the MAC-TEC CEO did not attempt to combine these various functions yet. He listed those he felt to be essential to each of the PPorP organizations. He deferred the formation of groups within each PPorP until the responsible executives were hired.

5. Next, he identified managers (vice presidents, directors, or whatever level was needed) for the three major businesses. Once the candidates had were hired, he gave them the task of forming the new businesses from the draft material he had developed. They worked initially as a group, and placed people, facilities, and organizations into groups. Once the initial groupings had been made, they worked out the further details with selected members of their new staffs. During this time, the CEO made a point of being readily available to resolve any resource conflicts.

At this juncture, the management decided that the systems manufacturing function and most of the Group 2 employees should stay centrally managed for now. A central operations organization was formed, along with a systems manufacturing group. The CEO chose executives to manage each. Each member of the management team was told that these central functions might be split apart later on. During the realignment process, a review was done on the size, cost, and accomplishments of the central activities. It was found that these functions tend to grow slowly, but inexorably, often without good cause, escaping the notice of general management until the next inevitable cost-cutting exercise.

The CEO insured that all involved management had ample opportunity to add ideas, comment, and hopefully agree to the organizational changes after they mulled over the good and the bad. Because of vested interests, it is too much to hope that the affected parties will all agree, but even the most radical may have constructive ideas. All managers were given plenty of latitude to offer alternatives.

6. Next, each executive and manager considered the advantages and disadvantages of each trial structure. Where the disadvantages appeared onerous, they tried arranging the functions differently. The marketing and preliminary development engineering groups seemed candidates for integration. **Marketers who work in technically oriented companies often have an engineering background and often want to be involved in the design of the products they sell. Engineers want to be involved with conceptual product definitions. A group composed of both functions can accomplish a great deal because they are not wasting time trying to one-up each other.**

Other candidates for realignment were the design engineering, manufacturing engineering, logistics, quality, and test equipment functions. The managers considered breaking up the finance function so that each PPorP organization had its own financial staff. The PPorP managers, wherever they may have reported in the old organization, would go with their respective P. This is a good time to examine each manager for his or her ability to manage employees. The managers then moved the staff into the newly formed organizations. A legal advisor and an administrator or two are all that are usually appropriate to retain in staff positions.

7. The management team led by the CEO critically examined the new structure. They reviewed the span of control exercised by each manager. The old rule that at most ten reporting employees or organizations are all a manager can deal with effectively seems to work very well. Furthermore, a competent manager should be able to supervise a minimum of at least five direct reporting positions. An exception to this rule may occur when the subordinate people or organizations are doing or managing wildly dissimilar and complex activities. When this happens, it is probably best to rethink the basic structure before proceeding, rather than creating a plethora of management positions. It may even be that the company is malformed and some products or services should be sold or terminated. **Note that each independent staff position should be counted as a direct reporting position for the purpose of determining the control span.** These staff employees and the inevitable conflicts with the line managers typically take a lot of time to control and resolve.

At this point, the MAC-TEC management arrived at an organization that looked like the one in the following figure:

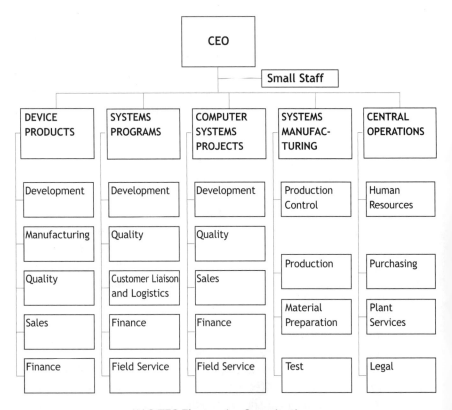

MAC-TEC Electronics Organization

The newly formed MAC-TEC Device Products business is shown in the figure below. The Systems Programs and Computer Systems Projects businesses are similarly configured.

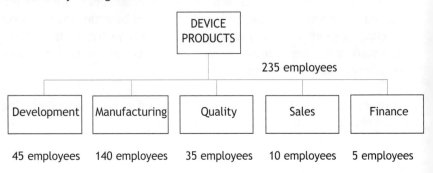

The New Device Products Organization

The Device Development Group is shown in the figure below.

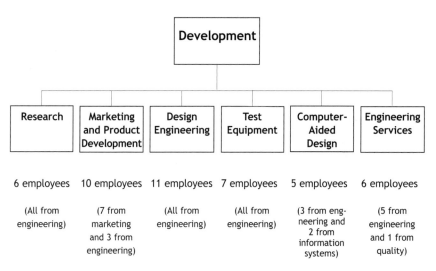

The New Device Development Organization

It was decided that classical marketing, product specification, device design, and test equipment design would be done under the direction of the development manager. Furthermore, the development group should have the resources and authority to specify and procure computer systems without approval from any central function, subject only to the review and approval of the Device Products executive.

Research activities were placed into a separate small organization to provide a degree of autonomy that would encourage the researchers to concentrate on new process development. The test equipment and computer-aided design groups could have been placed within the design engineering organization, forcing another level of management, but they were kept separate during this round of restructuring.

The device products executive decided that the sales function would remain separate from the marketing function. MAC-TEC's external sales were made principally through distributors and dealers working on commission, markup, and incentives. The sales group was well qualified to handle this part of the business, and the marketing group's involvement was minimal. However, managing common issues like co-op advertising might later be a problem. While the marketing group was responsible for the advertising program, the sales group would continue to deal with distributors for the co-op dollars, a source of possible conflict. Even within PPorP groups, there will be an infrequent overlap that must be dealt with at the next higher level.

When the MAC-TEC restructuring was complete, the CEO took pains to advise all MAC-TEC managers that job stability for everyone at MAC-TEC had a high priority, recognizing that instability in one part might well result in instability in all parts, including the management positions.

Bibliography

Drucker, P.F. 1974. *Effective Management Performance*. London: British Institute of Management.

Hayes, J.P. 1988. *Computer Architecture and Organization*. New York: Mc Graw-Hill.

Pollard, H.R. 1974. *Developments in Management Thought*. New York: Crane, Russak and Company.

Mc Murran, M.W. 1977. *Programming Microprocessors*. Blue Ridge Summit, PA: Tab Books.

Random House Webster's College Dictionary. 1997. Second Edition. New York: Random House.

Taylor, F.W. 1998. *The Principles of Scientific Management*. Norcross, GA: Engineering & Management Press.

Wren, D. 1987. *The Evolution of Management Thought*. Third Edition. New York: John Wiley and Sons.

Index

About EMP

ENGINEERING & MANAGEMENT PRESS (EMP) is the award-winning book publishing division of the Institute of Industrial Engineers (IIE). EMP was awarded the Association Trends Publishing Award for best book/manual in the soft cover category for *Manufacturing and the Internet* by Richard Mathieu (1996). EMP was also a finalist for the 1997 Small Press Book Awards in the Science/Engineering category for *Design of Experiments for Process Improvement and Quality Assurance*, and one of four finalists for the *Literary Marketplace* Corporate Achievement Award in the Professional Category (1996).

EMP was founded in 1981 as Industrial Engineering & Management Press (IE&MP). In 1995, IE&MP was reengineered as Engineering & Management Press. As both IE&MP and EMP, the press has a history of publishing successful titles, such as *Toyota Production System*, *Winning Manufacturing*, *Managing Quality in America's Most Admired Companies*, and *Beyond the Basics of Reengineering*.

Persons interested in submitting manuscripts should view our website at www.iienet.org or contact: Publisher, EMP, 25 Technology Park, Norcross, GA 30092.

About IIE

Founded in 1948, the INSTITUTE of Industrial Engineers (IIE) is comprised of more than 25,000 members throughout the United States and 89 other countries. IIE is the only international, nonprofit professional society dedicated to advancing the technical and managerial excellence of industrial engineers and all individuals involved in improving overall quality and productivity. IIE is committed to providing timely information about the profession to its membership, to professionals who practice industrial engineering skills, and to the general public.

IIE provides continuing education opportunities to members to keep them current on the latest technologies and systems that contribute to career advancement. The Institute provides products and services to aid in its endeavor, including professional magazines, journals, books, conferences, and seminars. IIE is constantly working to be the best available resource for information about the industrial engineering profession.

For more information about membership in IIE, please contact IIE Member and Customer Service at 800-494-0460 or 770-449-0460 or cs@iienet.org.

About the Author

The observations and advice Marshall W. Mc Murran provides in this book come from his thirty plus years managing engineers and other technical professionals. Mc Murran worked his way up through all levels of management, reaching the positions of Director of Engineering and Chief Engineer at Rockwell International. His career also includes several years as a consultant in signal processing. He holds a B.S. in Mathematics and Chemical Engineering from Oregon State University and a certificate in meteorology from UCLA, and is a Registered Professional Engineer (Control Systems) in California. Mc Murran is a flight instructor and commercial pilot.

Mc Murran is also the author of Programming Microprocessors.